Betty Crocker's
ULTIMATE COOKIE BOOK

Betty Crocker's
ULTIMATE COOKIE BOOK

MACMILLAN • USA

Macmillan General Reference
A Simon & Schuster Macmillan Company
1633 Broadway
New York, NY 10019-6785

Library of Congress Cataloging-in-Publication Data

Crocker, Betty.
   [Ultimate cookie book]
   Betty Crocker's ultimate cookie book.
      p.   cm.
   ISBN 0-13-084492-6
   1. Cookies. I. Title.
  TX772.C73   1992
  641.8′654—dc20   90-30659
                            CIP

Manufactured in the United States of America

10 9 8 7 6

First Edition

CONTENTS

INTRODUCTION

Cookies are not uniquely American, but our love for them seems to be exceptional. We're always dreaming up ways to improve or change them, dress them up or dress them down, make them crisper or chewier, simpler or more extravagant. Eighteenth-century colonists adapted their own recipes to work with the ingredients they found here, and the experimentation has scarcely slowed since. Although our word cookie is derived from the Dutch koekje, meaning "little cake," today it describes a much greater variety of baked sweets than little cakes.

This is our ultimate cookie book, a tremendous sampling of the most delicious cookies not only from America's past and present, but from around the world too. There are cookies for every taste in this collection, a feast for cookie lovers of all ages: old-fashioned cookies, new-fangled no-bake cookies, cookies for chocolate lovers, cookies filled with nuts or fruit and much, much more. An "ultimate" classic cookie is featured at the beginning of every chapter.

Whether you are an experienced or beginning baker, be sure to read through "All About Cookies" on pages 1–5. You can refer to the advice in this little "refresher course" of basic information whether you want extra help with a particular type of cookie or have a specific problem. We know that making cookies is one of the very nicest ways for beginning bakers to learn, and every recipe can be understood and made with complete confidence by the most novice of cooks. We know, too, that cookies are such pleasing and warm treats to cheer family and friends that you will turn to this book for a lifetime of wonderful baking.

THE BETTY CROCKER EDITORS

CHAPTER ONE

ALL ABOUT COOKIES

About Ingredients

Flour: Use either bleached or unbleached all-purpose flour. Many recipes also call for whole wheat flour. Drop cookies made with stone-ground flour may spread more and have a coarser texture than those made with regular whole wheat flour. The recipes in this book were not tested with self-rising flour. Too much flour makes cookies dry and tough; too little causes them to spread and lose their shape. Today's flours are presifted so no sifting is needed.

Rolled oats: Use either quick-cooking or old-fashioned rolled oats unless specified in recipe. Old-fashioned rolled oats make a chewier, slightly drier cookie. Quick-cooking oats are best for nonbaked recipes because they absorb moisture better and are less chewy.

Sugar: Sugar adds sweetness and color (by browning) and contributes to spreading. The higher the sugar-to-flour ratio in a recipe, the more tender and crisp the cookies will be.

Fat: Fats add tenderness and flavor to cookies. Butter and margarine both produce a crisper cookie than shortening and can be used interchangeably; butter gives a more buttery flavor and a crisper cookie than margarine. Use stick butter or margarine rather than tub or whipped, which contain more added water. When recipes call for shortening, use the solid type made from hydrogenated

vegetable oil. Shortening gives cookies a softer texture than margarine or butter, and the cookies can be somewhat drier and crumbly. Never substitute vegetable oil for a solid fat.

Cocoa: When recipes call for cocoa, use the unsweetened kind; do not use instant cocoa mix.

Leavening: Virtually all baking powder on the market today is double-acting. This means it begins acting when mixed with a liquid and is activated a second time when heated in the oven. Baking soda will react only with an acid such as buttermilk, lemon juice or molasses. If leavening is old or has been exposed to moisture, cookies made with it will be dense and flat.

Eggs: Eggs add richness, moisture and structure to cookies. Too many eggs can make cookies crumbly. All of the recipes in this book have been tested with large eggs.

Liquids: Liquids tend to make cookies crisper by making them spread more.

Equipment to Have on Hand

Measuring spoons, graduated measuring cups, liquid measuring cups, mixing bowls, a wooden spoon, a rubber scraper, flatware teaspoons and tablespoons, a hand beater or electric mixer, three or four cookie sheets, a timer, a wide spatula (to remove cookies to cooling racks) and cooling racks are just some of the equipment to have on hand.

Use cookie sheets at least two inches narrower and shorter than oven so heat will circulate around them. Shiny, bright sheets are best for delicate browning. Watch cookies carefully if using a sheet with a nonstick coating—cookies may brown quickly; follow manufacturers' directions as many suggest reducing the oven temperature by 25°. Consider using two cookie sheets, one stacked on top of the other for insulation, if cookie sheets are thin.

Measure Correctly

Graduated measuring spoons: Pour or scoop dry ingredients into spoon until full, then level off. Pour liquid into spoon until full.

Graduated measuring cups: Spoon flour or powdered sugar into cup, then level off with metal spatula or straight-edged knife. Do not tap cup or pack more into cup before leveling. Do not sift flour before measuring. Sift powdered sugar after measuring, if lumpy. Scoop granulated sugar into cup, then level off. To measure nuts, coconut and cut-up or small fruit, spoon into cup and pack down lightly. To measure brown sugar or shortening, spoon into cup and pack down firmly.

Liquid measuring cups: Pour in liquid to required level. Read the measurement at eye level.

Mixing

Use electric mixer when specified (speed and mixing time are given). Usually the sugars, fats and liquids are mixed together first, either by electric mixer according to directions, or by hand until ingredients are well combined. Then the dry ingredients are stirred in just until moistened. Air incorporated into the fat acts like a leavening. Cookies mixed by hand will be more compact and dense than cookies mixed with a mixer because there is less air beat into the fat. Do not overmix or cookies will be tough.

Shaping

Drop cookies: Spoon dough with a flatware spoon (not a measuring spoon) unless a level teaspoon or tablespoon is specified. Push dough onto cookie sheet with another spoon or rubber scraper. If cookies spread too much, chill dough before dropping onto sheet. (Incorrect oven temperature and warm cookie sheet can also cause spreading.)

Rolled cookies: Many recipes call for rolling dough on a floured surface to prevent sticking. If recipe calls for using pastry cloth and cloth-covered rolling pin, rub flour into cloths before rolling. Roll lightly and evenly. When dough requires chilling, roll only part of the dough at a time and keep the remainder refrigerated. Dip cutters in flour and shake off excess before cutting. Cut cookies close together to avoid rerolling (rerolled dough will be a little tougher). Lift cut cookies to cookie sheet with spatula to avoid stretching.

Molded cookies: Take the time to make the cookies uniform so they will not only look nice but bake evenly. If dough is too soft to work with, cover and refrigerate about one hour or until firm. Chill wrapped rolls of refrigerator cookie dough until firm enough to slice easily with a sharp knife. Cut into thickness specified in recipe. If cut too thin, the cookies will be hard; if too thick, they will be soft.

Pressed cookies: Do not refrigerate dough for pressed cookies (unless specified in recipe) or it will be too stiff to push through the press. Test the dough for consistency before adding all the flour. Put a small amount of dough in the cookie press and squeeze out. The dough should be soft and pliable but not crumbly. If dough is too stiff, add one egg yolk. If too soft, add flour one tablespoon at a time until the correct consistency is achieved. Hold press so that it rests on cookie sheet (unless using ribbon plate). Squeeze gently and raise press from cookie sheet when enough dough has been released to form a cookie. For ribbon plate, hold press at an angle to cookie sheet and release enough dough to form length of ribbon desired.*

Bar cookies: Spread or press dough evenly to sides of pan. Use correct pan size; bars baked in a pan that is too large can become hard from overbaking and, baked in a pan that is too small, they may be doughy in center from underbaking. Cool bars in pan before cutting to prevent crumbling, unless recipe specifies cutting while warm.

Greasing

Use shortening when greasing cookie sheets, and only grease if specified in recipe. Regrease sheets as needed during baking.

Baking

Place cookie dough on greased or ungreased cookie sheet as directed. Bake a "test" cookie. If it spreads more than desired, add one to two tablespoons

flour to the dough. If it is too dry, add one to two tablespoons milk. Always place dough on a cool cookie sheet—it will spread too much if placed on a hot one. Make all cookies on each cookie sheet the same size to ensure uniform baking. We recommend baking one cookie sheet at a time, using middle rack.** Check at the minimum bake time. Watch cookies carefully while baking, as even one minute can make a difference. Cookies become crisper or harder the longer they are baked.

Doneness

Although bake times are stated in every recipe, a doneness test is also given. Sometimes the color of the cookie may be the best test (until light brown, or until edges begin to brown, for example). Sometimes, especially if the dough is dark, a color change is hard to see. Then, the test might be until almost no indentation remains when touched in center. After baking one or two sheets you should get a feel for an approximate bake time. Use that time as your first check, but always use the doneness test as your final check.

Cooling

Some cookies need to be removed from the cookie sheet immediately after baking to prevent sticking. Some need to cool slightly (one to two minutes) before removing to allow them time to set; otherwise, they will fall apart. The larger the cookie, the longer the cooling time. Follow recipes carefully. Always cool cookies on wire cooling racks to allow

*There are several types of cookie presses on the market today. For best results, follow manufacturers' directions.

**If you wish to bake two sheets at once, remember to switch sheets halfway through baking.

the air to flow all around the cookies to prevent sogginess. Cool cookies completely before frosting unless instructed to frost warm.

Storing

Store unbaked cookie dough tightly covered in the refrigerator for up to twenty-four hours. To store refrigerator cookie dough in the freezer, wrap shaped dough in vaporproof freezer wrap (waxed plastic wrap or aluminum foil). Label and freeze for up to six months. When ready to bake, slice frozen dough with a sharp knife.

Store crisp cookies in a loosely covered container. This allows the flow of air to keep them crisp. If they soften, heat in a 300° oven three to five minutes to recrisp. Store soft cookies in a tightly covered container to prevent moisture loss. A piece of bread or apple (replaced frequently) in the container helps to keep the cookies soft.

Frosted cookies can be frozen for up to three months. Freeze them uncovered until they are firm, then pack in single layer in a container lined with freezer wrap. Unfrosted cookies can be frozen for up to twelve months. Layer in a container lined with freezer wrap with wrap between each layer. Seal the lining, close container, label and freeze. Let frozen cookies stand uncovered on serving plate about twenty minutes before serving.

Mailing

Bars baked in disposable foil pans and sturdy drop, refrigerator or molded cookies are best for mailing. These cookies are less fragile and travel better than crisp, thin cookies. Take the climate of your cookies' destination into account when making your selection. Wrap cookies separately or back to back in pairs in waxed paper, plastic wrap, aluminum foil or small plastic bags. Pack wrapped cookies in a coffee can or sturdy box, filling the container as full as practical and padding the top with crushed paper or packing material to prevent shaking or breakage. Pack containers in a corrugated or fiberboard packing box. For filler, use crumpled newspaper, shredded paper or packing material. Seal packing box with strapping or reinforced tape at least two inches wide. Wrap securely in brown paper if desired. Address in large print directly on package or on a gummed mailing label. Cover address with transparent tape to protect it from blurring. Do not use string as it can get snagged and torn off, perhaps damaging the package.

Creative Decorating Ideas

A decorating bag and assorted decorating tips make cookie decorating a snap. A good substitute, however, is a heavy plastic freezer bag with 1/8 inch of one bottom corner snipped off to make a writing tip. Use this Decorator's Frosting recipe (page 5) for spreading or piping.

Rolled cookie dough is probably the most versatile dough for making special-occasion cookies. It can be cut into any shape and decorated before or after baking. Use the Egg Yolk Paint or Cookie Paint (page 5) to paint light-colored, unbaked dough. Dark dough can be decorated with candies or raisins, or with frosting after baking.

Decorator's Frosting: Beat 2 cups powdered sugar, ½ teaspoon vanilla and about 2 tablespoons half-and-half or milk until smooth and of spreading consistency. Frosting can be tinted with food color. Makes enough to frost 3 to 5 dozen cookies.

Egg Yolk Paint: Blend 1 egg yolk and ¼ teaspoon water. Divide mixture among several custard cups. Tint with food colors to desired brightness. Paint on cookie dough before baking. If paint thickens on standing, add a few drops of water.

Cookie Paint: Tint small amounts of evaporated milk with different food colors. Paint on cookie dough before baking.

Special-Occasion Cutouts

Place cards: Roll dough ¼ inch thick. Cut into rectangles, 2¼ × 1½ inches. Cut triangles from dough to make stands, slightly shorter than height of place card and tapered to form an angle less than 90°. Bake as directed in recipe. Attach triangle to back of place card with frosting.

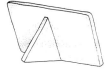

Cut triangles from dough to make angled stand.   *Attach triangles to back of place cards with frosting.*   *Decorate as desired.*

Gift tags: Roll dough ⅛ to 3/16 inch thick. Cut into tag shapes, about 2 × 1 inch. Make holes with straw for string or ribbon to thread through.

Bake as directed in recipe. Attach cooled cookies to packages just before giving them to recipients.

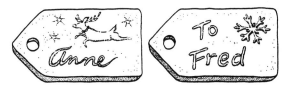

Make holes with straw before baking.   *Decorate as desired.*

Greeting cards: Roll dough ⅛ to 3/16 inch thick. Cut into desired card sizes, being sure to make two pieces of each size. Make two holes with straw on left side of dough, about 1½ inches apart (holes must be in same place on "matching" pieces of dough). Bake as directed in recipe. Tie cooled card pieces together with ribbon.

Cut matching pieces of dough: make matching holes on left side with straw before baking.   *Decorate as desired.*   *Tie cooled cards together with ribbon.*

Transplants: Use two different colored doughs to make mix-and-match inserts from one cookie into another. Cut desired designs with cookie cutters. Use smaller cutters to cut out and switch inserts made from doughs of different colors. Bake as directed in recipe.

CHAPTER TWO
THE ALL-AMERICAN CHOCOLATE CHIP COOKIE

▼▲▼▲▼▲▼▲▼▲▼▲▼▲▼▲▼▲▼▲▼▲▼▲▼▲▼▲▼▲

There were many American recipes for cookies before Ruth Wakefield baked the first Toll House cookie, but somehow cookies have never been the same since. For years the original chocolate chip cookie formula kept us very happy. But home bakers have created marvelous variations over the years, and we've been busy too. Here are our favorite chocolate chip cookie recipes.

▼▲▼▲▼▲▼▲▼▲▼▲▼▲▼▲▼▲▼▲▼▲▼▲▼▲▼▲▼▲

THE ULTIMATE CHOCOLATE CHIP COOKIE

¾ cup granulated sugar

¾ cup packed brown sugar

1 cup margarine or butter, softened

1 egg

2¼ cups all-purpose or whole wheat flour

1 teaspoon baking soda

½ teaspoon salt

1 cup coarsely chopped nuts

1 package (12 ounces) semisweet chocolate chips (2 cups)

Heat oven to 375°. Mix sugars, margarine and egg in large bowl. Stir in flour, baking soda and salt. (Dough will be stiff.) Stir in nuts and chocolate chips.

Drop dough by rounded tablespoonfuls about 2 inches apart onto ungreased cookie sheet. Bake 8 to 10 minutes or until light brown. (Centers will be soft.) Cool slightly; remove from cookie sheet. **About 4 dozen cookies.**

The Ultimate Chocolate Chip Cookie

DELUXE CHOCOLATE CHIP COOKIES

Bake these large, luscious cookies just the way you like them—a few minutes less for gooey, chewy centers, a few minutes longer for crisper cookies.

1 cup packed brown sugar

¾ cup granulated sugar

1 cup margarine or butter, softened

1 teaspoon vanilla

2 eggs

2½ cups all-purpose flour

¾ teaspoon baking soda

¾ teaspoon salt

1 cup chopped walnuts

12 ounces semisweet or milk chocolate, coarsely chopped, or semisweet chocolate chips (2 cups) or 1 package (10 ounces) chocolate deluxe baking pieces

Heat oven to 375°. Beat sugars and margarine in large bowl on medium speed about 3 minutes or until fluffy. Beat in vanilla and eggs. Stir in flour, baking soda and salt. Stir in nuts and chocolate.

Drop dough by level ¼ cupfuls about 2 inches apart onto ungreased cookie sheet. Flatten slightly with fork. Bake 11 to 14 minutes or until edges are light brown. (Centers will be soft.) Cool 3 to 4 minutes; remove from cookie sheet. **About 22 cookies.**

SOUR CREAM—MILK CHOCOLATE CHIP COOKIES

1½ cups sugar

½ cup sour cream

¼ cup margarine or butter, softened

¼ cup shortening

1 teaspoon vanilla

1 egg

2¼ cups all-purpose flour

½ teaspoon baking soda

¼ teaspoon salt

1 package (11.5 ounces) milk chocolate chips

Heat oven to 350°. Mix sugar, sour cream, margarine, shortening, vanilla and egg in large bowl. Stir in remaining ingredients except chocolate chips. Stir in chocolate chips.

Drop dough by rounded tablespoonfuls about 2 inches apart onto ungreased cookie sheet. Bake 12 to 14 minutes or until set and just beginning to brown. Cool slightly; remove from cookie sheet. **About 3½ dozen cookies.**

Sour Cream—Vanilla Milk Chip Cookies: Substitute vanilla milk chips for the milk chocolate chips.

CHOCOLATE-ORANGE—CHOCOLATE CHIP COOKIES

1 cup sugar

⅔ cup margarine or butter, softened

1 tablespoon grated orange peel

1 egg

1½ cups all-purpose flour

⅓ cup cocoa

¼ teaspoon salt

¼ teaspoon baking powder

¼ teaspoon baking soda

1 cup chopped pecans

1 package (6 ounces) semisweet chocolate chips (1 cup)

⅓ cup sugar

1 teaspoon grated orange peel

Heat oven to 350°. Mix 1 cup sugar, the margarine, 1 tablespoon grated orange peel and the egg in large bowl. Stir in flour, cocoa, salt, baking powder and baking soda. Stir in pecans and chocolate chips.

Roll dough into 1½-inch balls. Mix ⅓ cup sugar and 1 teaspoon grated orange peel. Roll balls of dough in sugar mixture. Place about 3 inches apart on ungreased cookie sheet. Flatten to about ½ inch thickness with bottom of glass. Bake 9 to 11 minutes or until set. Cool slightly; remove from cookie sheet. **About 2½ dozen cookies.**

CHOCOLATE CHIP SHORTBREAD COOKIES

1 cup margarine or butter, softened

¾ cup packed brown sugar

2 cups all-purpose flour

1 cup miniature semisweet chocolate chips

Heat oven to 350°. Mix margarine and brown sugar in large bowl until well blended. Stir in flour. Stir in chocolate chips.

Roll dough into 1¼-inch balls. Place about 3 inches apart on ungreased cookie sheet. Flatten to about ½-inch thickness with greased bottom of glass dipped in sugar. Bake 12 to 14 minutes or until set. Cool slightly; remove from cookie sheet. **About 3 dozen cookies.**

Deluxe Chocolate Chip Cookies (page 8), Chocolate-Orange–Chocolate Chip Cookies (page 9), Sour Cream–Milk Chocolate Chip Cookies (page 8)

GIANT TOFFEE–CHOCOLATE CHIP COOKIES

Mini chips make these big toffee-flavored cookies look positively monstrous. Don't try to fit more than six cookies to a cookie sheet because they spread.

1 cup packed brown sugar

½ cup margarine or butter, softened

½ cup shortening

¼ cup honey

1 egg

2 cups all-purpose flour

1 teaspoon baking soda

½ teaspoon baking powder

¼ teaspoon salt

1 package (12 ounces) miniature semisweet chocolate chips

1 package (6 ounces) almond brickle chips

Heat oven to 350°. Mix brown sugar, margarine, shortening, honey and egg in large bowl. Stir in flour, baking soda, baking powder and salt. Stir in chocolate chips and brickle chips.

Drop dough by level ¼ cupfuls about 2 inches apart onto ungreased cookie sheet. Bake 12 to 14 minutes or until edges are golden brown. (Centers will be soft.) Cool 3 to 4 minutes; remove from cookie sheet. **About 1½ dozen cookies.**

Regular Toffee–Chocolate Chip Cookies: Drop dough by rounded tablespoonfuls 2 inches apart onto ungreased cookie sheet. Bake 10 to 12 minutes or until golden brown. **About 4 dozen cookies.**

Some people like chocolate chip cookies crisp and golden brown, others like them chewy and just kissed with color. For chewy cookies, reduce the minimum bake time by one to two minutes, adjusting for your personal preference.

Giant Toffee–Chocolate Chip Cookies

The All-American Chocolate Chip Cookie

CHOCOLATE CHIP SANDWICH COOKIES

These cookies prove that too much of a good thing is simply wonderful. Try filling them with cream cheese, jam, peanut butter or chocolate-hazelnut spread. (If using cream cheese, store filled cookie sandwiches in the refrigerator.) The cookies will soften because they absorb moisture from the filling.

1¼ cups packed brown sugar

½ cup margarine or butter, softened

1 egg

1¼ cups all-purpose flour

¼ teaspoon baking soda

⅛ teaspoon salt

1 cup miniature semisweet chocolate chips

Chocolate Frosting (page 27)

Heat oven to 350°. Lightly grease cookie sheet. Mix brown sugar, margarine and egg in large bowl. Stir in flour, baking soda and salt. Stir in chocolate chips.

Drop dough by level teaspoonfuls about 2 inches apart onto cookie sheet. (Dough will flatten and spread.) Bake 8 to 10 minutes or until golden brown. Cool slightly; remove from cookie sheet. Cool completely. Prepare Chocolate Frosting. Spread 1 teaspoon frosting on bottoms of half of the cookies. Top with remaining cookies. **About 4 dozen sandwich cookies.**

CHOCOLATE-COVERED PEANUT—CHOCOLATE CHIP COOKIES

1 cup sugar

½ cup shortening

½ cup margarine or butter, softened

1 teaspoon vanilla

1 egg

1¾ cups all-purpose flour

½ teaspoon baking soda

¼ teaspoon salt

1 cup chocolate-covered peanuts

1 cup milk chocolate chips

Heat oven to 375°. Mix sugar, shortening, margarine, vanilla and egg in large bowl. Stir in flour, baking soda and salt. Stir in peanuts and chocolate chips.

Drop dough by rounded tablespoonfuls about 2 inches apart onto ungreased cookie sheet. Bake 10 to 12 minutes or until edges are golden brown. (Centers will be soft.) Cool slightly; remove from cookie sheet. **About 3½ dozen cookies.**

Chocolate-covered Raisin—Chocolate Chip Cookies: Substitute chocolate-covered raisins for the chocolate-covered peanuts.

Chocolate Chip Sandwich Cookies

FRESH MINT–CHOCOLATE CHIP COOKIES

Fresh mint is a delicious surprise in these unusually delicate cookies—perfect with a cup of tea.

1⅓ cups sugar

¾ cup margarine or butter, softened

1 tablespoon finely chopped mint leaves*

1 egg

2 cups all-purpose flour

1 teaspoon baking soda

½ teaspoon salt

1 package (10 ounces) mint chocolate chips

Heat oven to 350°. Mix sugar, margarine, mint leaves and egg in large bowl. Stir in flour, baking soda and salt. Stir in chocolate chips.

Drop dough by rounded tablespoonfuls about 2 inches apart onto ungreased cookie sheet. Bake 11 to 13 minutes or until golden brown. Cool slightly; remove from cookie sheet. **About 3½ dozen cookies.**

Mini Fresh Mint–Chocolate Chip Cookies: Drop dough by level teaspoonfuls onto ungreased cookie sheet. Bake 6 to 8 minutes or until golden brown. **About 10½ dozen cookies.**

*¼ teaspoon mint extract can be substituted for the chopped mint leaves.

> To make chocolate chip cookie bars, press Ultimate Chocolate Chip Cookie dough into ungreased jelly roll pan, 15½ × 10½ × 1 inch. Bake 15 to 20 minutes or until golden brown; cool. 48 bars.

Fresh Mint–Chocolate Chip Cookies

INSIDE-OUT–CHOCOLATE CHIP COOKIES

Creamy white chips in dark, chocolaty cookies—these chocolate chip cookies have been turned inside-out!

1 cup granulated sugar	2½ cups all-purpose flour
¾ cup packed brown sugar	½ cup cocoa
¾ cup margarine or butter, softened	1 teaspoon baking soda
½ cup shortening	¼ teaspoon salt
2 eggs	1½ cups vanilla milk chips
1 teaspoon vanilla	1 cup chopped nuts

Heat oven to 350°. Mix sugars, margarine, shortening, eggs and vanilla in large bowl. Stir in flour, cocoa, baking soda and salt. Stir in vanilla milk chips and nuts.

Drop dough by rounded tablespoonfuls about 2 inches apart onto ungreased cookie sheet. Bake 10 to 12 minutes or until set. Cool slightly; remove from cookie sheet. **About 4½ dozen cookies.**

Double Chocolate–Chocolate Chip Cookies: Substitute semisweet or milk chocolate chips for the vanilla milk chips.

Inside-out–Chocolate Chip Cookies

Chapter Three
Drop Cookies

▀▄▀▄▀▄▀▄▀▄▀▄▀▄▀▄▀▄▀▄▀▄▀▄▀▄▀▄▀▄▀▄▀▄▀

Making cookies by the drop method is about as easy as it gets. Space the cookies evenly, and use the same amount of dough for each so they bake evenly. When a teaspoon or tablespoon is called for to measure out amounts of dough, don't use a measuring spoon but rather a flatware teaspoon or tablespoon.

▀▄▀▄▀▄▀▄▀▄▀▄▀▄▀▄▀▄▀▄▀▄▀▄▀▄▀▄▀▄▀▄▀▄▀

THE ULTIMATE
Oatmeal Cookie

⅔ cup granulated sugar

⅔ cup packed brown sugar

½ cup margarine or butter, softened

½ cup shortening

1 teaspoon baking soda

1 teaspoon ground cinnamon

1 teaspoon vanilla

½ teaspoon baking powder

½ teaspoon salt

2 eggs

3 cups quick-cooking or old-fashioned oats

1 cup all-purpose flour

1 cup raisins or 2 cups (12 ounces) semisweet chocolate chips, if desired

Heat oven to 375°. Mix all ingredients except oats, flour and raisins in large bowl. Stir in oats, flour and raisins. Drop dough by rounded tablespoonfuls about 2 inches apart onto ungreased cookie sheet. Bake 9 to 11 minutes or until light brown. Immediately remove from cookie sheet. **About 3 dozen cookies.**

▀▄▀▄▀▄▀▄▀▄▀▄▀▄▀▄▀▄▀▄▀▄▀▄▀▄▀▄▀▄▀▄▀▄▀

The Ultimate Oatmeal Cookie, Frosted Banana Oaties (page 26)

DOUBLE OAT COOKIES

1 cup margarine or butter, softened

1 cup packed brown sugar

1 teaspoon vanilla

1 egg white

1¼ cups all-purpose flour

1 cup quick-cooking or old-fashioned oats

1 cup oat bran

½ teaspoon ground cinnamon

¼ teaspoon salt

¼ teaspoon baking powder

Heat oven to 350°. Mix margarine, brown sugar, vanilla and egg white in large bowl. Stir in remaining ingredients.

Drop dough by rounded tablespoonfuls about 2 inches apart onto ungreased cookie sheet. Bake 10 to 12 minutes or until golden brown. Cool slightly; remove from cookie sheet. **About 3 dozen cookies.**

TOASTED OATMEAL COOKIES

Toasting oats gives them unique flavor, very nice with the walnuts. Bake these cookies a minute or two less for soft cookies, a minute or two longer for crisp cookies.

2½ cups quick-cooking or old-fashioned oats

1 cup chopped walnuts

1½ cups packed brown sugar

1 cup margarine or butter, softened

1 teaspoon vanilla

1 egg

1 cup all-purpose flour

1 teaspoon baking soda

¼ teaspoon salt

Heat oven to 350°. Spread oats and walnuts in ungreased jelly roll pan, 15½ × 10½ × 1 inch. Bake 15 to 20 minutes, stirring occasionally, until light brown. Cool.

Mix brown sugar, margarine, vanilla and egg in large bowl. Stir in oat mixture and remaining ingredients.

Drop dough by rounded tablespoonfuls about 2 inches apart onto ungreased cookie sheet. Bake 8 to 10 minutes or until golden brown. Cool slightly; remove from cookie sheet. **About 3½ dozen cookies.**

Double Oat Cookies, Toasted Oatmeal Cookies

GIANT HONEY AND OAT COOKIES

Cholesterol-free and fun.

1½ cups sugar	4 cups quick-cooking or old-fashioned oats
¾ cup margarine, softened, or shortening	2 cups all-purpose flour
⅔ cup honey	1 teaspoon baking soda
3 egg whites	½ teaspoon salt

Heat oven to 350°. Grease cookie sheet. Mix sugar, margarine, honey and egg whites in large bowl. Stir in remaining ingredients.

Drop dough by level ¼ cupfuls about 3 inches apart onto cookie sheet. Bake 11 to 14 minutes or until edges are light brown. (Centers will be soft.) Cool 3 to 4 minutes. Remove from cookie sheet. **1½ dozen cookies.**

OATMEAL LACIES

Here is a delicate oatmeal cookie, flat, with crisp edges and a chewy center.

1½ cups quick-cooking oats	2 tablespoons all-purpose flour
⅔ cup packed brown sugar	1 teaspoon baking powder
⅓ cup margarine or butter, melted	⅛ teaspoon salt
¼ cup milk	1 egg

Heat oven to 350°. Grease and flour cookie sheet or line with cooking parchment paper. Mix all ingredients. Drop dough by level tablespoonfuls about 3 inches apart onto cookie sheet. Bake 8 to 10 minutes or until edges are golden brown. Cool slightly; remove from cookie sheet or cool completely and remove from parchment paper. **About 2½ dozen cookies.**

Giant Honey and Oat Cookies, Chocolate Drop Cookies (page 27)

FROSTED BANANA OATIES

Think of these as moist little banana cakes.

1 cup sugar

1 cup mashed very ripe bananas (2 to 3 medium)

¾ cup margarine or butter, softened

1 egg

2½ cups quick-cooking or old-fashioned oats

1 cup all-purpose flour

½ teaspoon salt

½ teaspoon baking soda

½ teaspoon ground cinnamon

¼ teaspoon ground allspice

Vanilla Frosting (below)

Heat oven to 350°. Grease cookie sheet. Mix sugar, banana, margarine and egg in large bowl. Stir in remaining ingredients except Vanilla Frosting.

Drop dough by rounded tablespoonfuls about 2 inches apart onto cookie sheet. Bake 10 to 12 minutes or until edges are golden brown and almost no indentation remains when touched in center.

Cool slightly; remove from cookie sheet. Cool completely. Prepare Vanilla Frosting and spread on cookies. **About 3½ dozen cookies.**

VANILLA FROSTING

3 cups powdered sugar, sifted

⅓ cup margarine or butter, softened

2 to 3 tablespoons milk

1½ teaspoons vanilla

Mix all ingredients until smooth and of desired consistency.

CHOCOLATE-OATMEAL CHEWIES

1½ cups sugar

1 cup margarine or butter, softened

¼ cup milk

1 egg

2⅔ cups quick-cooking or old-fashioned oats

1 cup all-purpose flour

½ cup cocoa

½ teaspoon salt

½ teaspoon baking soda

Heat oven to 350°. Mix sugar, margarine, milk and egg in large bowl. Stir in remaining ingredients.

Drop dough by rounded tablespoonfuls about 2 inches apart onto ungreased cookie sheet. Bake 10 to 12 minutes or until almost no indentation remains when touched in center. Cool slightly; remove from cookie sheet. **About 3½ dozen cookies.**

CHOCOLATE DROP COOKIES

1 cup sugar	1 egg
½ cup margarine or butter, softened	1¾ cups all-purpose flour
⅓ cup buttermilk	½ teaspoon baking soda
1 teaspoon vanilla	½ teaspoon salt
2 ounces unsweetened chocolate, melted and cooled	1 cup chopped nuts
	Chocolate Frosting (below)

Heat oven to 400°. Grease cookie sheet. Mix sugar, margarine, buttermilk, vanilla, chocolate and egg in large bowl. Stir in flour, baking soda, salt and nuts.

Drop dough by rounded tablespoonfuls about 2 inches apart onto cookie sheet. Bake 9 to 11 minutes or until almost no indentation remains when touched in center. Immediately remove from cookie sheet. Cool completely. Prepare Chocolate Frosting and spread on cookies. **About 3 dozen cookies.**

CHOCOLATE FROSTING

2 ounces unsweetened chocolate	2 cups powdered sugar
2 tablespoons margarine or butter	3 tablespoons hot water

Heat chocolate and margarine in 2-quart saucepan over low heat until melted; remove from heat. Stir in powdered sugar and water until smooth. (If frosting is too thick, add more water. If frosting is too thin, add more powdered sugar.)

FUDGY MACADAMIA COOKIES

1 cup sugar	1 egg
½ cup margarine or butter, softened	1 cup all-purpose flour
1 teaspoon vanilla	½ teaspoon baking powder
2 ounces unsweetened chocolate, melted and cooled	½ teaspoon salt
	1 cup chopped macadamia nuts

Heat oven to 350°. Mix sugar, margarine, vanilla, chocolate and egg in large bowl. Stir in remaining ingredients.

Drop dough by rounded tablespoonfuls about 2 inches apart onto ungreased cookie sheet. Bake 9 to 11 minutes or until almost no indentation remains when touched in center. Cool slightly; remove from cookie sheet. **About 2 dozen cookies.**

Frosted Cinnamon—Mocha Cookies

Enjoy these unusual treats after your favorite Mexican meal.

1 cup sugar

½ cup margarine or butter, softened

2 teaspoons freeze-dried instant coffee

1 egg

3 ounces unsweetened chocolate, melted and cooled

1¼ cups all-purpose flour

¼ cup milk

1 teaspoon ground cinnamon

½ teaspoon baking soda

¼ teaspoon salt

Mocha Frosting (below)

Heat oven to 350°. Mix sugar, margarine, instant coffee and egg in large bowl. Stir in chocolate. Stir in remaining ingredients except Mocha Frosting.

Drop dough by rounded tablespoonfuls about 2 inches apart onto ungreased cookie sheet. Bake 10 to 12 minutes or until almost no indentation remains when touched in center. Cool completely. Prepare Mocha Frosting and spread on cookies. **About 2½ dozen cookies.**

Mocha Frosting

1 teaspoon freeze-dried instant coffee

3 tablespoons hot water

2 ounces unsweetened chocolate

2 tablespoons margarine or butter

2 cups powdered sugar

2 to 3 teaspoons water

Dissolve instant coffee in 3 tablespoons hot water; reserve. Heat chocolate and margarine in 2-quart saucepan over low heat, stirring frequently, until melted; remove from heat. Stir in powdered sugar, the reserved coffee mixture and 2 to 3 teaspoons water until smooth and spreading consistency.

CHOCOLATE—PEANUT BUTTER NO-BAKES

1 package (6 ounces) semisweet chocolate
    chips (1 cup)

¼ cup light corn syrup

¼ cup peanut butter

2 tablespoons milk

1 teaspoon vanilla

2 cups quick-cooking oats

1 cup peanuts

Line cookie sheets with waxed paper. Heat chocolate chips, corn syrup, peanut butter, milk and vanilla in 3-quart saucepan over medium heat, stirring constantly, until chocolate is melted and mixture is smooth; remove from heat. Stir in oats and peanuts.

Drop mixture by rounded tablespoonfuls onto waxed paper. Refrigerate uncovered about 1 hour or until firm. Cover and refrigerate any remaining cookies. **About 2 dozen cookies.**

HONEY-ROASTED PEANUT CRISPS

These butterscotchy cookies are studded with sweet-salty peanuts.

1 cup packed brown sugar

½ cup margarine or butter, softened

½ cup shortening

1 teaspoon vanilla

1 egg

2 cups all-purpose flour

½ teaspoon baking powder

¼ teaspoon salt

2 cups honey-roasted peanuts

Heat oven to 375°. Mix brown sugar, margarine, shortening, vanilla and egg in large bowl. Stir in remaining ingredients.

Drop dough by rounded tablespoonfuls about 2 inches apart onto ungreased cookie sheet. Flatten with greased bottom of glass dipped in sugar. Bake 9 to 11 minutes or until golden brown. Cool slightly; remove from cookie sheet. **About 4 dozen cookies.**

DOUBLE PEANUT COOKIES

1 cup peanut butter

¾ cup granulated sugar

¾ cup packed brown sugar

½ cup margarine or butter, softened

2 eggs

1½ cups all-purpose flour

1 teaspoon baking soda

1½ cups chopped unsalted dry roasted peanuts

Heat oven to 375°. Mix peanut butter, sugars, margarine and eggs in large bowl. Stir in flour and baking soda. Stir in peanuts. (Dough will be stiff.)

Drop dough by rounded tablespoonfuls about 2 inches apart onto ungreased cookie sheet. Bake 8 to 10 minutes or until light brown. Cool slightly; remove from cookie sheet. **About 4½ dozen cookies.**

WHOLE WHEAT—FRUIT DROPS

A wonderful lunch-box cookie.

¾ cup packed brown sugar

½ cup plain yogurt

¼ cup margarine or butter, softened

1 tablespoon grated orange peel

½ teaspoon vanilla

1 egg

1½ cups whole wheat flour

½ teaspoon baking soda

¼ teaspoon baking powder

1 package (6 ounces) diced dried fruits and raisins (about 1¼ cups)

Heat oven to 375°. Mix brown sugar, yogurt, margarine, orange peel, vanilla and egg in large bowl. Stir in remaining ingredients.

Drop dough by rounded tablespoonfuls about 2 inches apart onto ungreased cookie sheet. Bake 11 to 13 minutes or until light brown. Remove from cookie sheet. **About 2½ dozen cookies.**

Whole Wheat—Date Cookies: Decrease brown sugar to ½ cup. Substitute 1 package (8 ounces) chopped dates for the diced dried fruits and raisins.

Double Peanut Cookies

Drop Cookies

WHOLE WHEAT–HONEY COOKIES

½ cup packed brown sugar	1 egg
½ cup margarine or butter, softened	2 cups whole wheat flour
½ cup honey	½ teaspoon salt
½ teaspoon vanilla	½ teaspoon baking soda

Heat oven to 375°. Mix brown sugar, margarine, honey, vanilla and egg in large bowl. Stir in remaining ingredients.

Drop dough by rounded tablespoonfuls about 2 inches apart onto ungreased cookie sheet. Bake 9 to 11 minutes or until light brown around edges. Remove from cookie sheet. **About 2 dozen cookies.**

Honey-Cinnamon Cookies: Stir in ½ teaspoon ground cinnamon with the flour. Mix 2 tablespoons granulated sugar and ½ teaspoon ground cinnamon; sprinkle over cookies immediately after removing from oven.

WHOLE WHEAT MELTAWAYS

1 cup margarine or butter, softened	¾ cup whole wheat flour
1 cup powdered sugar	¼ teaspoon salt
2 teaspoons vanilla	Powdered sugar
1 cup all-purpose flour	

Heat oven to 375°. Mix margarine, 1 cup powdered sugar and the vanilla in large bowl. Stir in flours and salt.

Drop dough by rounded tablespoonfuls about 2 inches apart onto ungreased cookie sheet. Bake 12 to 15 minutes or until almost no indentation remains when touched in center. Cool slightly; remove from cookie sheet. Cool completely. Lightly sprinkle with powdered sugar. **About 2 dozen cookies.**

Whole Wheat Meltaways, Whole Wheat–Honey Cookies

BROWN SUGAR DROPS

2 cups packed brown sugar

½ cup shortening

½ cup margarine or butter, softened

½ cup milk

2 eggs

3½ cups all-purpose flour

1 teaspoon baking soda

½ teaspoon salt

Butter Frosting (below)

Heat oven to 400°. Mix brown sugar, shortening, margarine, milk and eggs in large bowl. Stir in remaining ingredients except Butter Frosting.

Drop dough by rounded tablespoonfuls about 2 inches apart onto ungreased cookie sheet. Bake 9 to 11 minutes or until almost no indentation remains when touched in center. Cool slightly; remove from cookie sheet. Cool completely. Prepare Butter Frosting and spread on cookies. **About 5 dozen cookies.**

BUTTER FROSTING

4 cups powdered sugar

½ cup margarine or butter, melted

2 teaspoons vanilla

2 to 4 tablespoons milk

Beat all ingredients until smooth and spreading consistency.

Applesauce–Brown Sugar Drops: Substitute 1 cup applesauce for the milk. Stir in 1½ teaspoons ground cinnamon, ¼ teaspoon ground cloves and 1 cup raisins. **About 5 dozen cookies.**

Cherry–Brown Sugar Drops: Stir in 1 cup chopped, well-drained maraschino cherries. Press cherry half in each cookie before baking if desired. Omit frosting. **About 6 dozen cookies.**

Whole Wheat–Brown Sugar Drops: Substitute 2 cups whole wheat flour for 2 cups of the all-purpose flour. Add 1 cup chopped pecans. Press pecan half in each cookie before baking if desired. Omit frosting. **About 5 dozen cookies.**

Soft Molasses Cookies (page 36), Brown Sugar Drops, Sour Cream Cookies (page 37)

SOFT MOLASSES COOKIES

1 cup sugar

½ cup margarine or butter, softened

½ cup shortening

¾ cup sour cream

½ cup light molasses

1 egg

3 cups all-purpose flour

1½ teaspoons baking soda

1 teaspoon ground ginger

1 teaspoon ground cinnamon

½ teaspoon salt

Heat oven to 375°. Mix sugar, margarine, shortening, sour cream, molasses and egg in large bowl. Stir in remaining ingredients.

Drop dough by rounded tablespoonfuls about 2 inches apart onto ungreased cookie sheet. Bake 9 to 11 minutes or until almost no indentation remains when touched in center. Cool slightly; remove from cookie sheet. Sprinkle with sugar while warm if desired. **About 4 dozen cookies.**

BUTTERMILK-SPICE DROPS

1 cup sugar

½ cup margarine or butter, softened

1 egg

½ cup buttermilk

½ teaspoon vanilla

2 cups all-purpose flour

1 cup raisins

1 teaspoon ground cinnamon

½ teaspoon baking soda

½ teaspoon salt

½ teaspoon ground ginger

¼ teaspoon ground cloves

Spice Frosting (below)

Heat oven to 375°. Mix sugar, margarine and egg in large bowl. Stir in buttermilk and vanilla. Stir in remaining ingredients except Spice Frosting.

Drop dough by rounded tablespoonfuls about 2 inches apart onto ungreased cookie sheet. Bake 9 to 11 minutes or until almost no indentation remains when touched in center. Cool completely. Prepare Spice Frosting and spread on cookies. **About 2½ dozen cookies.**

SPICE FROSTING

1¾ cups powdered sugar

3 tablespoons margarine or butter, softened

5 to 6 teaspoons milk

¼ teaspoon ground cinnamon

⅛ teaspoon ground ginger

Dash of ground cloves

Mix all ingredients until smooth and spreading consistency.

SOUR CREAM COOKIES

1½ cups packed brown sugar

1 cup sour cream

½ cup shortening

1 teaspoon vanilla

2 eggs

2¾ cups all-purpose flour

½ teaspoon salt

½ teaspoon baking soda

1 cup chopped pecans, if desired

Browned Butter Frosting (below)

Heat oven to 375°. Mix brown sugar, sour cream, shortening, vanilla and eggs in large bowl. Stir in remaining ingredients except Browned Butter Frosting.

Drop dough by rounded teaspoonfuls about 2 inches apart onto ungreased cookie sheet. Bake 8 to 10 minutes or until almost no indentation remains when touched in center. Cool slightly; remove from cookie sheet. Cool completely. Prepare Browned Butter Frosting and spread on cookies. **About 6 dozen cookies.**

BROWNED BUTTER FROSTING

⅓ cup margarine or butter

2 cups powdered sugar

2 to 3 tablespoons hot water

1½ teaspoons vanilla

Heat margarine in 1 quart saucepan over low heat until golden brown; remove from heat. Stir in remaining ingredients until smooth and spreading consistency.

Applesauce Cookies: Substitute ¾ cup applesauce for sour cream. Stir in 1 teaspoon ground cinnamon, ¼ teaspoon ground cloves and 1 cup raisins with the flour.

Coconut–Sour Cream Cookies: Substitute shredded coconut for the pecans.

Salted Peanut–Sour Cream Cookies: Substitute salted peanuts for the pecans.

Spice–Sour Cream Cookies: Mix ½ cup granulated sugar, 1 teaspoon ground cinnamon and ¼ teaspoon ground cloves; sprinkle over cookies before baking. Omit frosting.

SPICY PUMPKIN-DATE COOKIES

This soft, date-filled cookie is just right for a crisp autumn day.

1 cup sugar

½ cup margarine or butter

1 cup canned pumpkin

2 eggs

2 cups all-purpose flour

2 teaspoons baking powder

2 teaspoons ground cinnamon

½ teaspoon ground nutmeg

½ teaspoon ground ginger

¼ teaspoon ground cloves

1 cup chopped dates

½ cup chopped walnuts

Heat oven to 375°. Beat sugar and margarine in large bowl on medium speed about 3 minutes or until light and fluffy. Beat in pumpkin and eggs. Stir in remaining ingredients. Drop dough by rounded teaspoonfuls about 2 inches apart onto ungreased cookie sheet. Bake 8 to 10 minutes or until edges are set. Immediately remove from cookie sheet. **About 4 dozen cookies.**

OLD-FASHIONED DATE DROP COOKIES

1½ cups packed brown sugar

1 cup margarine or butter

1 tablespoon grated orange peel

1 teaspoon vanilla

2 eggs

2 cups all-purpose flour

1 cup quick-cooking oats

1 teaspoon baking soda

¼ teaspoon salt

1 package (8 ounces) chopped dates

½ cup chopped pecans

Heat oven to 350°. Grease cookie sheet. Mix brown sugar, margarine, orange peel, vanilla and eggs in large bowl. Stir in flour, oats, baking soda and salt. Stir in dates and pecans.

Drop dough by rounded teaspoonfuls about 2 inches apart onto cookie sheet. Bake 8 to 10 minutes or until light brown. Remove from cookie sheet. **About 6 dozen cookies.**

BRANDIED FRUIT DROPS

¾ cup packed brown sugar

½ cup margarine or butter

⅓ cup brandy

2 eggs

2 cups all-purpose flour

2 teaspoons baking powder

1 teaspoon ground cardamom

½ teaspoon ground cinnamon

½ teaspoon ground nutmeg

1 cup chopped pecans

1 cup dried apricots, chopped

½ cup currants

½ cup golden raisins

Heat oven to 350°. Grease cookie sheet. Mix brown sugar, margarine, brandy and eggs in large bowl. Stir in flour, baking powder, cardamom, cinnamon and nutmeg. Stir in remaining ingredients.

Drop dough by rounded teaspoonfuls about 2 inches apart onto cookie sheet. Bake 9 to 11 minutes or until cookies are light brown. Remove from cookie sheet. **About 5 dozen cookies.**

OLD-FASHIONED RUM-RAISIN COOKIES

1 cup raisins

½ cup water

¼ cup rum*

½ cup margarine or butter, softened

¾ cup sugar

1 egg

1¾ cups all-purpose flour

½ teaspoon baking soda

½ teaspoon baking powder

¼ teaspoon salt

Heat raisins, water and rum to boiling in 1-quart saucepan; reduce heat. Simmer uncovered 20 to 30 minutes or until raisins are plump and liquid is evaporated. Cool raisins 30 minutes.

Heat oven to 375°. Beat margarine and sugar in large bowl on medium speed about 3 minutes or until fluffy. Beat in egg. Stir in remaining ingredients, including undrained raisins.

Drop dough by rounded tablespoonfuls about 2 inches apart onto ungreased cookie sheet. Bake 9 to 11 minutes or until light brown. Remove from cookie sheet. **About 2½ dozen cookies.**

¼ cup water and 1 teaspoon rum extract can be substituted for the rum.

Brandied Fruit Drops (page 39), Old-fashioned Rum-Raisin Cookies (page 39)

LEMON-LIME COOKIES

After grating the peel from citrus fruits, use the "bald" fruits for lemonade and the like.

1 cup sugar

⅔ cup shortening

1 tablespoon grated lemon peel

2 teaspoons grated lime peel

2 tablespoons lemon juice

1 tablespoon lime juice

1 egg

1¾ cups all-purpose flour

½ teaspoon baking powder

½ teaspoon baking soda

½ teaspoon salt

Lemon-Lime Frosting (below)

Heat oven to 375°. Mix sugar, shortening, lemon peel, lime peel, lemon juice, lime juice and egg in large bowl. Stir in remaining ingredients except Lemon-Lime Frosting.

Drop dough by rounded tablespoonfuls about 2 inches apart onto ungreased cookie sheet. Bake 11 to 13 minutes or until edges are golden brown. Cool slightly; remove from cookie sheet. Cool completely. Prepare Lemon-Lime Frosting and spread on cookies. **About 2 dozen cookies.**

LEMON-LIME FROSTING

2 cups powdered sugar

2 tablespoons margarine or butter, softened

1 tablespoon lemon juice

1 teaspoon grated lime peel

2 to 3 teaspoons water

Mix all ingredients until smooth and of spreading consistency.

Orange Cookies: Substitute 2 tablespoons grated orange peel for the lemon and lime peels and ¼ cup orange juice for the lemon and lime juices in the cookie dough. Substitute 1 teaspoon grated orange peel for the lime peel and about 2 tablespoons orange juice for the lemon juice and water in the frosting.

Lemon-Lime Cookies, Pineapple Puffs (page 44)

PINEAPPLE PUFFS

1½ cups sugar

½ cup margarine or butter, softened

½ cup sour cream or plain yogurt

1 egg

1 can (8¼ ounces) crushed pineapple, undrained

3½ cups all-purpose flour

1 teaspoon baking soda

1 teaspoon vanilla

½ teaspoon salt

½ cup chopped almonds

Vanilla Frosting (below)

Heat oven to 375°. Mix sugar, margarine, sour cream, egg and pineapple in large bowl. Stir in remaining ingredients except Vanilla Frosting.

Drop dough by teaspoonfuls about 2 inches apart onto ungreased cookie sheet. Bake 8 to 10 minutes or until almost no indentation remains when touched in center. Immediately remove from cookie sheet. Cool completely. Prepare Vanilla Frosting and spread on cookies. **About 6½ dozen cookies.**

VANILLA FROSTING

2 cups powdered sugar

2 to 3 tablespoons milk

1 teaspoon vanilla

Mix ingredients until smooth and of spreading consistency.

APPLESAUCE-GRANOLA COOKIES

1 cup packed brown sugar

½ cup shortening

1 teaspoon vanilla

1 egg

½ cup applesauce

2 cups all-purpose flour

2 cups granola

½ teaspoon baking soda

½ teaspoon salt

Heat oven to 375°. Mix brown sugar, shortening, vanilla and egg in large bowl. Stir in applesauce. Stir in remaining ingredients.

Drop dough by rounded tablespoonfuls about 2 inches apart onto ungreased cookie sheet. Bake 11 to 13 minutes or until almost no indentation remains when touched in center. Cool slightly; remove from cookie sheet. **About 3½ dozen cookies.**

BANANA-GINGER JUMBLES

Fresh ginger gives the brightest ginger flavor.

1 cup packed brown sugar

½ cup margarine or butter, softened

½ cup shortening

1 tablespoon grated fresh gingerroot or 1 tea-spoon ground ginger*

2 eggs

1 cup mashed ripe bananas (about 2 large)

¼ cup milk

3 cups all-purpose flour

1 teaspoon baking powder

¾ teaspoon salt

Heat oven to 375°. Mix brown sugar, margarine, shortening, gingerroot and eggs in large bowl. Stir in bananas and milk. Stir in remaining ingredients.

Drop dough by rounded tablespoonfuls about 2 inches apart onto ungreased cookie sheet. Bake 9 to 11 minutes or until almost no indentation remains when touched in center. Remove from cookie sheet. Sprinkle with powdered sugar while warm if desired. **About 3½ dozen cookies.**

*If using ground ginger, stir in with flour.

Whole Wheat–Banana-Ginger Cookies: Substitute 2¾ cups whole wheat flour for the all-purpose flour.

Banana-Raisin Cookies: Omit gingerroot; stir in 1 cup golden raisins with flour.

PASTEL MINT DROPS

These fun cookies call for the pastel mint drop candies found at candy shops. If you can find the mini-mint drops, use them as a shortcut to chopping the candies.

¾ cup sugar

½ cup vegetable oil

2 eggs

1 teaspoon vanilla

2 cups all-purpose flour

½ cup chopped pastel mint drop candies

2 teaspoons baking powder

½ teaspoon salt

Heat oven to 375°. Mix sugar, oil, eggs and vanilla in large bowl. Stir in remaining ingredients.

Drop dough by rounded teaspoonfuls about 2 inches apart onto ungreased cookie sheet. Bake 8 to 10 minutes or until edges are light brown. Remove from cookie sheet. **About 5 dozen cookies.**

Drop Cookies

GINGER-PECAN CHEWS

These molasses-flavored cookies feature luscious bits of candied ginger.

½ cup sugar

½ cup margarine or butter, softened

½ cup molasses

1 jar (2.7 ounces) crystallized ginger, chopped (about ½ cup)

1 egg

2 cups all-purpose flour

1 teaspoon ground ginger

½ teaspoon baking soda

½ teaspoon salt

½ cup chopped pecans

Heat oven to 375°. Mix sugar, margarine, molasses, crystallized ginger and egg in large bowl. Stir in remaining ingredients.

Drop dough by rounded tablespoonfuls about 2 inches apart onto ungreased cookie sheet. Press pecan half in each cookie if desired. Bake 12 to 14 minutes or until almost no indentation remains when touched in center. Immediately remove from cookie sheet. **2½ to 3 dozen cookies.**

CORNMEAL CRISPIES

¾ cup sugar

1 cup margarine or butter, softened

1 egg

1¼ cups all-purpose flour

1 cup yellow cornmeal

1 teaspoon baking powder

1 teaspoon grated lemon peel

½ teaspoon salt

Heat oven to 350°. Mix sugar, margarine and egg in large bowl. Stir in remaining ingredients.

Drop dough by rounded teaspoonfuls about 2 inches apart onto ungreased cookie sheet. Bake 10 to 12 minutes or until edges are light brown. Cool slightly; remove from cookie sheet. **About 5 dozen cookies.**

Ginger-Pecan Chews

Coconut Meringue Cookies

For a successful meringue, both beaters and mixing bowl must be free of any trace of grease. Beat in the sugar gradually and continue beating to stiff peaks. The Nut Meringue Cookies are a little flatter than the coconut ones (when the oil from the nuts hits the meringue, the batter falls slightly).

4 egg whites (½ cup)

1¼ cups sugar

¼ teaspoon salt

½ teaspoon vanilla

2½ cups shredded or flaked coconut

Heat oven to 325°. Lightly grease cookie sheet or line with cooking parchment paper. Beat egg whites in large bowl on high speed until foamy. Gradually beat in sugar. Continue beating until stiff and glossy. (Do not underbeat.) Stir in salt, vanilla and coconut.

Drop mixture by heaping teaspoonfuls about 2 inches apart onto cookie sheet. Bake 15 to 20 minutes or until set and light brown. Cool 5 minutes. Carefully remove from cookie sheet. **About 3 dozen cookies.**

Nut Meringue Cookies: Substitute 2 cups finely chopped nuts for the coconut.

Poppy Drop Cookies

1 cup sugar

1 cup margarine or butter, softened

1 egg

1¾ cups all-purpose flour

2 tablespoons poppy seed

1 teaspoon baking powder

¼ teaspoon salt

Poppy Seed Glaze (below)

Heat oven to 375°. Mix sugar, margarine and egg in large bowl. Stir in remaining ingredients except Poppy Seed Glaze.

Drop dough by rounded tablespoonfuls about 2 inches apart onto ungreased cookie sheet. Bake 10 to 12 minutes or until edges are golden brown. Cool slightly; remove from cookie sheet. Cool completely. Prepare Poppy Seed Glaze and drizzle on cookies. **About 2 dozen cookies.**

Poppy Seed Glaze

1½ cups powdered sugar

2 tablespoons milk

1 teaspoon poppy seed

½ teaspoon vanilla

Mix all ingredients until smooth.

Coconut Meringue Cookies

Drop Cookies

49

CHAPTER FOUR
ROLLED COOKIES

▛▜▛▜▛▜▛▜▛▜▛▜▛▜▛▜▛▜▛▜▛▜▛▜

O**ne of the nice things about rolled cookies is that they will wait until you are ready to bake them. Because the dough can always be refrigerated (and can be frozen, too), they're very convenient. And we love them because they present lots of opportunity for creativity. Simple cookies are ideal for teaching the beginning baker how to handle a rolling pin. Any of these delicious cookies are the place to start for cozy afternoons spent on the pleasures of decorating.**

▛▜▛▜▛▜▛▜▛▜▛▜▛▜▛▜▛▜▛▜▛▜▛▜

THE ULTIMATE
SUGAR COOKIE

1½ cups powdered sugar

1 cup margarine or butter, softened

1 egg

1 teaspoon vanilla

½ teaspoon almond extract

2½ cups all-purpose flour

1 teaspoon baking soda

1 teaspoon cream of tartar

Granulated sugar

Mix powdered sugar and margarine in large bowl. Stir in egg, vanilla and almond extract. Stir in flour, baking soda and cream of tartar. Cover and refrigerate about 2 hours or until firm.

Heat oven to 375°. Roll half of dough at a time ⅛ inch thick on lightly floured surface. Cut into desired shapes. Place on ungreased cookie sheet; sprinkle with granulated sugar. Bake 7 to 8 minutes or until light brown. Remove from cookie sheet. **About 5 dozen 2- to 2½-inch cookies.**

▛▜▛▜▛▜▛▜▛▜▛▜▛▜▛▜▛▜▛▜▛▜▛▜

The Ultimate Sugar Cookie, Yogurt Stack Cookies (page 57)

SOUR CREAM–SUGAR COOKIES

This sugar cookie is more tender and cakelike than the crisp Ultimate Sugar Cookie, page 51.

1 cup sugar

⅓ cup margarine or butter, softened

¼ cup shortening

½ teaspoon lemon extract

1 egg

2⅔ cups all purpose flour

1 teaspoon baking powder

½ teaspoon baking soda

½ teaspoon salt

⅔ cup sour cream

Sugar

Heat oven to 375°. Mix 1 cup sugar, the margarine, shortening, lemon extract and egg in large bowl. Stir in flour, baking powder, baking soda, salt and sour cream. Roll one-third of dough at a time ¼ inch thick on well-floured cloth-covered surface. Cut into desired shapes with 2½-inch cookie cutter. Place about 2 inches apart on ungreased cookie sheet. Sprinkle lightly with sugar. Bake 7 to 8 minutes or until almost no indentation remains when touched. **About 3 dozen cookies.**

SUGAR COOKIE TARTS

2 cups sugar

1 cup shortening

¾ cup margarine or butter, softened

2 teaspoons vanilla

1 egg

3½ cups all-purpose flour

1 teaspoon baking powder

¼ teaspoon salt

Cream Cheese Spread (below)

Toppings (sliced fresh fruit, miniature chocolate chips, chopped pecans or jam and toasted sliced almonds)

Heat oven to 375°. Mix sugar, shortening, margarine, vanilla and egg in large bowl. Stir in flour, baking powder and salt. Roll half of dough at a time ¼ inch thick on lightly floured surface. Cut into 3-inch rounds. Place 2 inches apart on ungreased cookie sheet. Bake 10 to 12 minutes or until light brown. Cool slightly; remove from cookie sheet. Cool completely. Prepare Cream Cheese Spread. Spread about 2 teaspoons over each cookie. Arrange toppings on spread. Refrigerate any remaining cookies. **About 2½ dozen cookies.**

CREAM CHEESE SPREAD

½ cup sugar

1 teaspoon vanilla

1 package (8 ounces) cream cheese, softened

Mix ingredients until smooth.

Sugar Cookie Tarts

CREAM WAFERS

For variety, tint portions of the filling different colors

2 cups all-purpose flour

1 cup margarine or butter, softened

⅓ cup whipping (heavy) cream

Sugar

Creamy Filling (below)

Mix flour, margarine and whipping cream. Cover and refrigerate about 1 hour or until firm. Heat oven to 375°. Roll one-third of dough at a time ⅛ inch thick on floured surface. (Keep remaining dough refrigerated until ready to roll.) Cut into 1½-inch rounds. Generously cover large piece waxed paper with sugar. Using spatula, transfer rounds to waxed paper. Turn each round to coat both sides. Place on ungreased cookie sheet. Prick each round with fork about 4 times.

Bake 7 to 9 minutes or just until set but not brown. Remove from cookie sheet. Cool completely. Prepare Creamy Filling. Put cookies together in pairs with about ½ teaspoon filling each. **About 5 dozen sandwich cookies.**

CREAMY FILLING

¾ cup powdered sugar

¼ cup margarine or butter, softened

1 teaspoon vanilla

Food color, if desired

Mix all ingredients until smooth. Add few drops water if necessary.

CREAM SQUARES

2 eggs

1 cup sugar

1 cup whipping (heavy) cream

4 cups all-purpose flour

3 teaspoons baking powder

1 teaspoon salt

Beat eggs in large bowl until foamy. Gradually beat in sugar. Stir in whipping cream. Stir in flour, baking powder and salt. Cover and refrigerate about 2 hours or until firm.

Heat oven to 375°. Grease cookie sheet. Roll half of dough at a time into rectangle, 12 × 8 inches, on floured surface. Cut into 2-inch squares. Place 2 inches apart on cookie sheet. Make two ½-inch cuts on all sides of each square. Bake 10 to 13 minutes or until edges are light brown. Remove from cookie sheet. **About 4 dozen cookies.**

Cream Wafers, Cream Squares

YOGURT STACK COOKIES

1 cup sugar	1 teaspoon baking powder
½ cup margarine or butter, softened	½ teaspoon baking soda
½ cup shortening	¼ teaspoon salt
½ cup plain yogurt	Yogurt Frosting (below)
1 egg	⅓ cup fruit preserves (any flavor)
3 cups all-purpose flour	

Mix sugar, margarine and shortening in large bowl. Stir in yogurt and egg. Stir in flour, baking powder, baking soda and salt. Cover and refrigerate about 2 hours or until firm.

Heat oven to 375°. Roll half of dough at a time ⅛ inch thick on floured surface. Cut into 2-inch rounds. Place 2 inches apart on ungreased cookie sheet. Bake 6 to 8 minutes or until light brown. Remove from cookie sheet. Cool completely. Prepare Yogurt Frosting and spread 1 cookie with ½ teaspoon frosting. Top with second cookie; spread with ½ teaspoon preserves. Top with third cookie. Repeat with remaining cookies, frosting and preserves. Store tightly covered in refrigerator. **About 20 stack cookies.**

YOGURT FROSTING

1 cup powdered sugar	1 tablespoon margarine or butter, softened
2 tablespoons plain yogurt	¼ teaspoon vanilla

Mix all ingredients until smooth.

BUTTERSCOTCH SHORTBREAD

If you prefer shortbread cutouts, use a 2-inch cookie cutter.

½ cup margarine or butter, softened	¼ cup granulated sugar
½ cup shortening	2¼ cups all-purpose flour
½ cup packed brown sugar	1 teaspoon salt

Heat oven to 300°. Mix margarine, shortening and sugars in large bowl. Stir in flour and salt. (Dough will be dry and crumbly. Use hands to mix completely.) Roll dough into rectangle, 15 × 7½ inches, on lightly floured surface. Cut into 1½-inch squares. Place about 1 inch apart on ungreased cookie sheet. Bake about 25 minutes or until set. (These cookies brown very little and the shape does not change.) Remove from cookie sheet. **About 4 dozen cookies.**

Butterscotch Shortbread

Rolled Cookies

CHOCOLATE SHORTBREAD

As an alternative to the frosted spiderweb design described below, drizzle straight lines of chocolate across the white frosting; draw a wooden pick across the lines, alternating directions.

2 cups powdered sugar	4 ounces semisweet chocolate, melted and cooled
1½ cups margarine or butter	
3 cups all-purpose flour	½ teaspoon shortening
¾ cup cocoa	Creamy Frosting (below)
2 teaspoons vanilla	

Heat oven to 325°. Beat powdered sugar and margarine in large bowl until light and fluffy. Stir in flour, cocoa and vanilla.

Roll half of dough at a time ½ inch thick on lightly floured surface. Cut into 3-inch rounds. Place 2 inches apart on ungreased cookie sheet. Bake 9 to 11 minutes or until firm. (Do not let cookies get dark brown.) Remove from cookie sheet. Cool completely.

Mix chocolate and shortening until smooth. Prepare Creamy Frosting and spread each cookie with about 1 teaspoon. Immediately drizzle chocolate mixture on frosting making 3 concentric circles. Starting at center, draw a toothpick 5 to 6 times through chocolate circles to make spiderweb design. Let stand until chocolate is firm. **About 4 dozen cookies.**

CREAMY FROSTING

3 cups powdered sugar	1½ teaspoons vanilla
⅓ cup margarine or butter, softened	About 2 tablespoons milk

Mix powdered sugar and margarine in medium bowl. Stir in vanilla and milk. Beat until smooth and of spreading consistency.

CHOCOLATE-GLAZED GRAHAM CRACKERS

1 cup shortening	½ teaspoon baking powder
½ cup packed brown sugar	¼ teaspoon salt
¼ cup honey	½ cup semisweet chocolate chips
2 cups whole wheat flour	1 tablespoon shortening

Heat oven to 375°. Mix 1 cup shortening, the brown sugar and honey in large bowl. Stir in flour, baking powder and salt.

Roll half of dough at a time ⅛ inch thick on lightly floured cloth-covered surface. Cut into 2½-inch rounds. Place 1 inch apart on ungreased cookie sheet. Bake 7 to 9 minutes or until edges are firm. Cool slightly; remove from cookie sheet. Cool completely. Heat and stir chocolate chips and 1 tablespoon shortening until melted and smooth. Drizzle over cookies. **About 4 dozen cookies.**

Honey—Graham Cracker Cookies: Prepare dough as directed. Cut into desired shapes with 2-to 3-inch cookie cutters; sprinkle with sugar. Omit chocolate.

MALTED MILK COOKIES

2 cups packed brown sugar

1 cup margarine or butter, softened

⅓ cup sour cream

2 eggs

2 teaspoons vanilla

4¾ cups all-purpose flour

¾ cup natural malted milk powder

2 teaspoons baking powder

½ teaspoon baking soda

½ teaspoon salt

Malted Milk Frosting (below)

Heat oven to 375°. Mix brown sugar, margarine, sour cream, eggs and vanilla in large bowl. Stir in flour, malted milk powder, baking powder, baking soda and salt.

Roll one-third of dough at a time ¼ inch thick on floured surface. Cut into 2½-inch rounds. Place about 2 inches apart on ungreased cookie sheet. Bake 10 to 11 minutes or until almost no indentation remains when touched in center. Immediately remove from cookie sheet. Cool completely. Prepare Malted Milk Frosting and spread on cookies. **About 5 dozen cookies.**

MALTED MILK FROSTING

½ cup packed brown sugar

¼ cup margarine or butter

4 to 5 tablespoons milk or half-and-half

3¾ cups powdered sugar

⅓ cup natural malted milk powder

½ teaspoon vanilla

Heat brown sugar, margarine and milk in 2-quart saucepan over medium heat until margarine is melted; remove from heat. Stir in remaining ingredients until smooth.

MORAVIAN GINGER COOKIES

⅓ cup molasses

¼ cup shortening

2 tablespoons packed brown sugar

1¼ cups all-purpose or whole wheat flour

¼ teaspoon salt

¼ teaspoon baking soda

¼ teaspoon baking powder

¼ teaspoon ground cinnamon

¼ teaspoon ground ginger

¼ teaspoon ground cloves

Dash of ground nutmeg

Dash of ground allspice

Easy Creamy Frosting (below)

Mix molasses, shortening and brown sugar in large bowl. Stir in remaining ingredients except Easy Creamy Frosting. Cover and refrigerate about 4 hours or until firm.

Heat oven to 375°. Roll half of dough at a time ⅛ inch thick or paper-thin on floured cloth-covered surface. Cut into 3-inch rounds with floured cutter. Place about ½ inch apart on ungreased cookie sheet. Bake ⅛-inch-thick cookies about 8 minutes, paper-thin cookies about 5 minutes or until light brown. Immediately remove from cookie sheet. Cool completely. Prepare Easy Creamy Frosting and spread on cookies. **About 1 dozen ⅛-inch-thick cookies or about 1½ dozen paper-thin cookies.**

EASY CREAMY FROSTING

1 cup powdered sugar

1 to 2 tablespoons half-and-half

½ teaspoon vanilla

Mix ingredients until of spreading consistency.

FROSTED SPICE COOKIES

2½ cups packed brown sugar

1 cup margarine or butter, softened

½ cup shortening

2 eggs

4½ cups all-purpose flour

2 teaspoons baking powder

1 teaspoon ground ginger

1 teaspoon ground cinnamon

1 teaspoon ground cloves

1 teaspoon ground nutmeg

½ teaspoon salt

Frosting (page 61)

Heat oven to 375°. Mix brown sugar, margarine, shortening and eggs in large bowl. Stir in remaining ingredients except Frosting.

Roll one-fourth of dough at a time ¼ inch thick on lightly floured surface. Cut into 2½-inch rounds. Place about 2 inches apart on ungreased cookie sheet. Bake 8 to 10 minutes or until light brown. Remove from cookie sheet. Cool completely. Prepare Frosting and spread on cookies. **About 4 dozen cookies.**

FROSTING

1 envelope unflavored gelatin

¾ cup cold water

1 cup granulated sugar

1½ cups powdered sugar

1 teaspoon baking powder

1 teaspoon vanilla

⅛ teaspoon salt

Sprinkle gelatin on cold water in 2-quart saucepan to soften. Stir in granulated sugar. Heat to rolling boil; reduce heat. Simmer uncovered 10 minutes. Pour hot mixture over powdered sugar in large bowl. Beat on medium speed about 2 minutes or until foamy. Beat in remaining ingredients on high speed until soft peaks form.

GINGERBREAD COOKIES

1 cup packed brown sugar

⅓ cup shortening

1½ cups dark molasses

⅔ cup cold water

7 cups all-purpose flour

2 teaspoons baking soda

2 teaspoons ground ginger

1 teaspoon salt

1 teaspoon ground allspice

1 teaspoon ground cloves

1 teaspoon ground cinnamon

Creamy Frosting (below)

Mix brown sugar, shortening, molasses and water in large bowl. Stir in remaining ingredients except Creamy Frosting. Cover and refrigerate about 2 hours or until firm.

Heat oven to 350°. Lightly grease cookie sheet. Roll one-fourth of dough at a time ¼ inch thick on floured surface. Cut with floured gingerbread cookie cutter or other favorite shaped cutter. Place about 2 inches apart on cookie sheet. Bake 10 to 12 minutes or until almost no indentation remains when touched in center. Remove from cookie sheet. Cool completely. Prepare Creamy Frosting and spread on cookies. **About 2½ dozen 5-inch gingerbread cookies or about 5 dozen 2½-inch cookies.**

CREAMY FROSTING

4 cups powdered sugar

5 tablespoons half-and-half

1 teaspoon vanilla

Food color, if desired

Mix all ingredients until smooth.

Gingerbread Cookies (page 61)

JOE FROGGERS

This is an old-time American cookie named, some say, for a New Englander known as "Uncle Joe" who made molasses cookies as large as the lily pads in his frog pond.

1 cup sugar	1½ teaspoons ground ginger
½ cup shortening	1 teaspoon baking soda
1 cup dark molasses	½ teaspoon ground cloves
½ cup water	½ teaspoon ground nutmeg
4 cups all-purpose flour	¼ teaspoon ground allspice
1½ teaspoons salt	Sugar

Mix 1 cup sugar, the shortening, molasses and water in large bowl. Stir in remaining ingredients except sugar. Cover and refrigerate about 2 hours or until firm.

Heat oven to 375°. Lightly grease cookie sheet. Roll one-fourth of dough at a time ¼ inch thick on well-floured cloth-covered surface. Cut into 3-inch rounds. Place about 1½ inches apart on cookie sheet. Sprinkle with sugar. Bake 10 to 12 minutes or until almost no indentation remains when touched in center. Remove from cookie sheet. **About 2½ dozen cookies.**

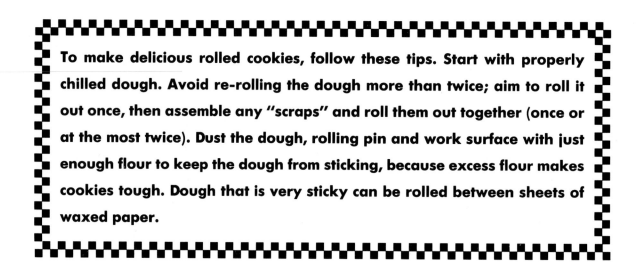

To make delicious rolled cookies, follow these tips. Start with properly chilled dough. Avoid re-rolling the dough more than twice; aim to roll it out once, then assemble any "scraps" and roll them out together (once or at the most twice). Dust the dough, rolling pin and work surface with just enough flour to keep the dough from sticking, because excess flour makes cookies tough. Dough that is very sticky can be rolled between sheets of waxed paper.

SUNSHINE COOKIES

Cornmeal adds a little crunch here.

½ cup margarine or butter, softened

¼ cup shortening

1 cup sugar

½ teaspoon almond extract

2 egg yolks

1¼ cups yellow cornmeal

1 cup all-purpose flour

1 teaspoon baking powder

¼ teaspoon salt

Heat oven to 400°. Mix margarine, shortening, sugar, almond extract and egg yolks in large bowl. Stir in cornmeal, flour, baking powder and salt.

Roll half of dough at a time ⅛ inch thick on lightly floured surface. Cut into desired shapes with 3-inch cutter. Place about 1 inch apart on ungreased cookie sheet. Bake 6 to 8 minutes or until very light brown. Immediately remove from cookie sheet. **About 4 dozen 3-inch cookies.**

PECAN CRISPS

2 cups sugar

¾ cup very finely chopped pecans

⅓ cup margarine or butter, softened

1 teaspoon vanilla

2 eggs

2¼ cups all-purpose flour

2½ teaspoons baking powder

¼ teaspoon salt

Heat oven to 375°. Mix sugar and pecans in large bowl. Reserve ¾ cup of sugar mixture. Stir margarine, vanilla and eggs into remaining sugar mixture. Stir in flour, baking powder and salt.

Roll dough into rectangle, 18 × 13 inches, on floured surface. Sprinkle generously with reserved sugar mixture. Press sugar mixture into dough with rolling pin. Cut dough diagonally in both directions every 2 inches with pastry wheel or knife to form diamonds. Place about 2 inches apart on ungreased cookie sheet. Bake 8 to 10 minutes or until golden brown. Immediately remove from cookie sheet. **About 4 dozen cookies.**

CHOCOLATE-PEANUT WINDMILLS

1 cup sugar

⅓ cup margarine or butter, softened

⅓ cup shortening

2 tablespoons milk

½ teaspoon vanilla

1 egg

2 ounces unsweetened chocolate, melted and cooled

1¾ cups all-purpose flour

1 teaspoon baking powder

⅛ teaspoon salt

½ cup finely chopped peanuts

Mix sugar, margarine, shortening, milk, vanilla and egg in large bowl. Stir in chocolate. Stir in flour, baking powder and salt. Cover and refrigerate about 2 hours or until firm.

Heat oven to 400°. Roll half of dough at a time into rectangle, 12 × 9 inches, on lightly floured cloth-covered surface. Sprinkle each rectangle with half of the peanuts. Gently press into dough. Cut dough into 3-inch squares. Place about 2 inches apart on ungreased cookie sheet. Cut squares diagonally from each corner almost to center. Fold every other point to center to resemble pinwheel. Bake about 6 minutes or until set. Cool 2 minutes; remove from cookie sheet. **About 2 dozen cookies.**

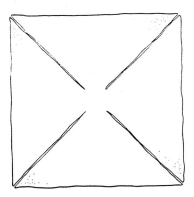

Cut squares diagonally from each corner almost to center.

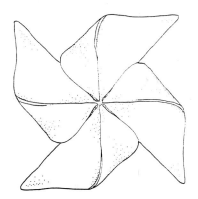

Fold every other point to center to resemble pinwheel.

Chocolate-Peanut Windmills, Malted Milk Cookies (page 59)

Rolled Cookies

Hungarian Poppy Seed Cookies

Lemon peel, clove and poppy seed often flavor Eastern European cookies. Look for commercially prepared poppy seed filling next to canned pie fillings at the supermarket.

½ cup margarine or butter

¼ cup granulated sugar

1 teaspoon grated lemon peel

1 egg

1¼ cups all-purpose flour

½ teaspoon baking soda

¼ teaspoon ground cloves

¾ cup poppy seed filling

Powdered sugar

Beat margarine and granulated sugar in large bowl until light and fluffy. Beat in lemon peel and egg. Stir in flour, baking soda and cloves. Roll dough between pieces of waxed paper into ¼-inch-thick rectangle, 12 × 10 inches. Refrigerate 30 minutes or until firm.

Heat oven to 350°. Grease cookie sheet. Remove waxed paper from one side of dough. Spread poppy seed filling to within ¼ inch of edges. Roll up tightly, beginning at 12-inch side, peeling off waxed paper as dough is rolled. Pinch edge of dough to seal well. Cut dough into ½-inch slices. Place on cookie sheet about 1 inch apart. Bake 10 to 12 minutes or until edges are light brown. Cool slightly; remove from cookie sheet. Sprinkle with powdered sugar. **About 3 dozen cookies.**

Hungarian Poppy Seed Cookies, Mint Ravioli Cookies (page 71)

CINNAMON-NUT CRISPS

2 cups all-purpose flour

½ cup sugar

¾ cup shortening

2 to 3 tablespoons water

3 tablespoons margarine or butter, softened

2 tablespoons sugar

1 teaspoon ground cinnamon

2 tablespoons very finely chopped nuts

Sugar

Heat oven to 375°. Mix flour and ½ cup sugar in large bowl. Cut shortening into flour mixture until particles are size of small peas. Add water, 1 tablespoon at a time, tossing with fork until mixture almost cleans side of bowl.

Roll dough into rectangle, 15 × 10 inches, on lightly floured cloth-covered surface. Spread with margarine. Mix 2 tablespoons sugar and the cinnamon; sprinkle evenly over margarine. Sprinkle nuts evenly over sugar mixture. Roll up tightly, beginning at 15-inch side. Cut crosswise into ¼-inch slices. Place about 2 inches apart on ungreased cookie sheet. Sprinkle with sugar. Bake 10 to 12 minutes or until golden brown. Remove from cookie sheet. **About 5 dozen cookies.**

Cinnamon-Nut Butterflies: Prepare and cut slices as directed. Place 2 slices side by side on cookie sheet, overlapping slightly; press to seal. Continue as directed—except bake 13 to 15 minutes.

DATE-NUT PINWHEELS

¾ pound pitted dates, finely chopped

⅓ cup granulated sugar

⅓ cup water

½ cup finely chopped nuts

1 cup packed brown sugar

¼ cup shortening

¼ cup margarine or butter, softened

1 egg

½ teaspoon vanilla

1¾ cups all-purpose flour

¼ teaspoon salt

Cook dates, granulated sugar and water in saucepan, stirring constantly, until slightly thickened; remove from heat. Stir in nuts; cool. Mix brown sugar, shortening, margarine, egg and vanilla in large bowl. Stir in flour and salt.

Roll half of dough at a time into rectangle, about 11 × 7 inches, on waxed paper. Spread half of the date-nut filling over each rectangle to within ¼ inch of long sides. Roll up tightly, beginning at long side. Pinch edge of dough to seal well. Wrap and refrigerate about 4 hours or until firm.

Heat oven to 400°. Cut rolls into ¼-inch slices. Place about 1 inch apart on ungreased cookie sheet. Bake 8 to 10 minutes or until light brown. Immediately remove from cookie sheet. **About 6 dozen cookies.**

Mint Ravioli Cookies

½ cup margarine or butter, softened

½ cup shortening

1 cup sugar

1 egg

2½ cups all-purpose flour

1 teaspoon baking powder

¼ teaspoon salt

3 dozen rectangular chocolate mints

Mix margarine, shortening, sugar and egg in large bowl. Stir in flour, baking powder and salt. Cover and refrigerate about 1 hour or until firm.

Heat oven to 400°. Roll half of dough into rectangle, 13 × 9 inches, on floured surface. Place mints on dough, forming 6 uniform rows of 6. Roll remaining dough into rectangle, 13 × 9 inches, on floured waxed paper. Place over mint-covered dough and remove waxed paper. Cut between mints with pastry wheel or knife and press edges with fork to seal. Bake on ungreased cookie sheet 7 to 9 minutes or until light brown. Remove from cookie sheet.

3 dozen cookies.

Place mints on dough, forming six rows of 6.

Place remaining dough over mint-covered dough; cut between mints.

Rolled Cookies

ALMOND-FILLED CRESCENTS

Use a metal spatula to pull the cut wedges of dough away from the circle.

1 cup powdered sugar

1 cup whipping (heavy) cream

2 eggs

3¾ cups all-purpose flour

1 teaspoon baking powder

½ teaspoon salt

1 can (8 ounces) almond paste

¾ cup margarine or butter, softened

Glaze (below)

Mix powdered sugar, whipping cream and eggs in large bowl. Stir in flour, baking powder and salt. (Dough will be stiff.) Cover and refrigerate about 1 hour or until firm.

Heat oven to 375°. Break almond paste into small pieces in medium bowl; add margarine. Beat on low speed until blended. Beat on high speed until fluffy (tiny bits of almond paste will remain).

Roll one-fourth of dough at a time into 10-inch circle on lightly floured surface. Spread one-fourth of almond paste mixture (about ½ cup) over circle. Cut into 12 wedges. Roll up, beginning at rounded edge. Place on ungreased cookie sheet with points underneath. Curve cookies to form crescents. Repeat with remaining dough and almond paste mixture. Bake 14 to 16 minutes or until golden brown. Remove from cookie sheet. Cool completely. Prepare Glaze and drizzle on crescents. **4 dozen crescents.**

GLAZE

1 cup powdered sugar

6 to 7 teaspoons milk

Mix until smooth and of desired consistency.

GLAZED CHOCOLATE POCKETS

It is easy to glaze all the cookies at one time—set them ¼ inch apart on a cooling rack over waxed paper and simply pour the glaze over them.

¼ cup powdered sugar

1 package (3 ounces) cream cheese, softened

½ teaspoon vanilla

⅓ cup flaked coconut

¾ cup margarine or butter, softened

⅔ cup granulated sugar

1 egg

2 cups all-purpose flour

⅓ cup cocoa

¼ teaspoon salt

Glaze (below)

Heat oven to 375°. Mix powdered sugar and cream cheese until thoroughly blended. Stir in vanilla and coconut; reserve filling. Mix margarine, granulated sugar and egg in large bowl. Stir in remaining ingredients except Glaze.

Roll dough into rectangle, 16 × 12 inches, on lightly floured cloth-covered surface. Cut into 4-inch squares. Cut squares in half diagonally to form triangles. Place 1 level teaspoon filling in center of each triangle; flatten slightly. Fold points of triangle to corner, and press edges to seal. Place on ungreased cookie sheet. Bake 10 to 12 minutes or until set. Remove from cookie sheet. Cool completely. Prepare Glaze and drizzle half on cookies. Add cocoa and milk to remaining glaze as directed in recipe. Drizzle on cookies. **2 dozen cookies.**

GLAZE

1 cup powdered sugar

4 to 6 teaspoons milk

1 tablespoon cocoa

1 to 2 teaspoons milk

Mix powdered sugar and 4 to 6 teaspoons milk in 2-cup liquid measure until of drizzling consistency. Drizzle about half over cookies by pouring from measuring cup. (About 3 tablespoons will remain.) Stir cocoa and 1 to 2 teaspoons milk into remaining glaze in cup.

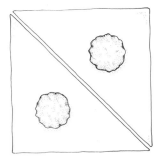

Cut squares in half diagonally to form triangles, and place filling in center of each triangle.

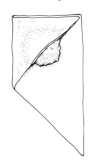

Fold points of triangle to corner.

Press edges to seal.

Rolled Cookies

PEACH TRIANGLES

Peach Filling (below)

1 cup sugar

½ cup shortening

2 eggs

2 cups all-purpose flour

1½ teaspoons baking powder

¼ teaspoon salt

Sugar

Heat oven to 375°. Prepare Peach Filling. Mix 1 cup sugar and shortening in large bowl. Stir in eggs. Stir in flour, baking powder and salt.

Roll half of dough at a time ⅛ inch thick on lightly floured cloth-covered surface. Cut into 3-inch rounds. Place 1 level teaspoon filling in center of each round. Bring three sides of each round together at center to form triangle. Pinch edges together to form slightly ridge. Place on ungreased cookie sheet. Sprinkle with sugar. Bake 9 to 12 minutes or until golden brown. Cool slightly; remove from cookie sheet. **About 4 dozen cookies.**

PEACH FILLING

⅔ cup peach preserves

½ cup finely chopped dried peaches

Combine ingredients.

RASPBERRY LOGS

1 cup granulated sugar

½ cup margarine or butter

¼ cup shortening

2 teaspoons vanilla

2 eggs

2¼ cups all-purpose flour

½ cup ground walnuts

1 teaspoon baking powder

¼ teaspoon salt

½ cup raspberry preserves

Powdered sugar

Mix granulated sugar, margarine, shortening, vanilla and eggs in large bowl. Stir in remaining ingredients except preserves and powdered sugar. Cover and refrigerate about 3 hours or until firm.

Heat oven to 375°. Roll half of dough at a time into 12-inch square on floured cloth-covered surface. Cut into rectangles, 3 × 2 inches. Place ½ teaspoon preserves ¼ inch from edges along one 3-inch side of each rectangle. Fold dough lengthwise over preserves. Seal edges with fork. Place on ungreased cookie sheet. Bake 8 to 10 minutes or until light brown. Remove from cookie sheet. Roll in powdered sugar while warm. **4 dozen cookies.**

TOFFEE MERINGUE STICKS

Shape the dough strips easily this way: Roll one-fourth of the dough into a rope about 10 inches long, then roll and flatten it into a 12 × 3-inch rectangle.

1 cup packed brown sugar	2½ cups all-purpose flour
⅓ cup margarine or butter, softened	¼ teaspoon salt
1 teaspoon vanilla	2 egg whites
1 egg yolk	½ cup granulated sugar
½ cup whipping (heavy) cream	1 package (6 ounces) almond brickle pieces

Mix brown sugar, margarine, vanilla and egg yolk in large bowl. Stir in whipping cream. Stir in flour and salt. Cover and refrigerate about 1 hour or until firm.

Heat oven to 375°. Roll one-fourth of dough at a time into strip, 12 × 3 inches, on floured surface. Place two strips at a time about 2 inches apart on ungreased cookie sheet.

Beat egg whites in medium bowl on high speed until foamy. Gradually beat in granulated sugar. Continue beating until stiff and glossy. Fold in brickle pieces. Spread one-fourth of the meringue over each strip of dough. Bake 12 to 14 minutes or until edges are light brown. Cool 10 minutes. Cut each strip crosswise into 1-inch sticks. Remove from cookie sheet. **About 4 dozen cookies.**

Hazelnut Meringue Sticks: Substitute granulated sugar for the brown sugar and ¾ cup (2.5 ounces) ground hazelnuts for the almond brickle pieces.

CHOCOLATE-CHERRY STRIPE COOKIES

1½ cups sugar

½ cup shortening

½ cup margarine or butter, softened

1 teaspoon vanilla

1 egg

3 cups all-purpose flour

¼ teaspoon salt

¼ cup cocoa

2 tablespoons plus 1 teaspoon milk

⅓ cup finely chopped maraschino cherries, very well drained

Mix sugar, shortening, margarine, vanilla and egg in large bowl. Stir in flour and salt. Divide dough in half. Mix cocoa and milk into one half and cherries into the other half.

Roll cherry dough into rectangle, 10 × 8 inches, on floured surface, turning over occasionally so dough does not stick. Roll chocolate dough into rectangle, 10 × 8 inches, on waxed paper. Place chocolate rectangle on top of cherry rectangle and remove waxed paper. Cut in half lengthwise. Stack layers, being careful to alternate colors; repeat. Wrap and refrigerate about 2 hours or until firm.

Heat oven to 375°. Cut dough crosswise into ¼-inch slices. Place 2 inches apart on ungreased cookie sheet. Bake 9 to 11 minutes or until edges begin to brown. Cool slightly; remove from cookie sheet. **About 3½ dozen cookies.**

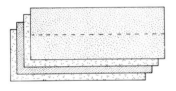

Stack layers of dough being careful to alternate colors.

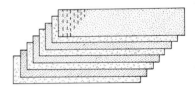

Repeat cutting lengthwise and stacking.

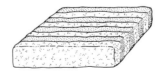

Cut dough crosswise into slices.

Toffee Meringue Sticks (page 75), Chocolate-Cherry Stripe Cookies

Rolled Cookies

CHAPTER FIVE
MOLDED COOKIES

▼▼▼▼▼▼▼▼▼▼▼▼▼▼▼▼▼▼▼▼▼▼▼▼▼▼▼▼▼▼▼▼▼

A**ll the cookies here are easily shaped (or "molded") by hand. Many molded cookies can be shaped and baked as soon as they have been mixed, with no delay. Others need to be refrigerated first. Lots of great cookies are molded such as filled bonbon cookies, cookies shaped into pinwheels and cookies in animal shapes.**

▼▼▼▼▼▼▼▼▼▼▼▼▼▼▼▼▼▼▼▼▼▼▼▼▼▼▼▼▼▼▼▼▼

THE ULTIMATE
REFRIGERATOR COOKIE

1 cup packed brown sugar

1 cup margarine or butter, softened

1 teaspoon vanilla

1 egg

3 cups all-purpose flour

1½ teaspoons ground cinnamon

½ teaspoon baking soda

½ teaspoon salt

⅓ cup chopped nuts

Mix brown sugar, margarine, vanilla and egg in large bowl. Stir in remaining ingredients. Shape dough into rectangle, 10 × 3 inches. Wrap and refrigerate about 2 hours or until firm.

Heat oven to 375°. Cut rectangles into ⅛-inch slices. Place 2 inches apart on ungreased cookie sheet. Bake 6 to 8 minutes or until light brown. Cool slightly; remove from cookie sheet. **About 6 dozen cookies.**

▼▼▼▼▼▼▼▼▼▼▼▼▼▼▼▼▼▼▼▼▼▼▼▼▼▼▼▼▼▼▼▼▼

The Ultimate Refrigerator Cookie, Chocolate-Peppermint Refrigerator Cookies (page 80)

MAPLE-NUT REFRIGERATOR COOKIES

¾ cup packed brown sugar

¾ cup margarine or butter, softened

¼ teaspoon maple extract

1½ cups all-purpose flour

1 teaspoon baking powder

¼ teaspoon salt

1 cup chopped pecans

Mix brown sugar, margarine and maple extract in large bowl. Stir in remaining ingredients. Shape into roll, 12 inches long. Wrap and refrigerate about 2 hours or until firm.

Heat oven to 375°. Cut roll into ¼-inch slices. Place 2 inches apart on ungreased cookie sheet. Bake 8 to 10 minutes or until edges are golden brown. Remove from cookie sheet. **4 dozen cookies.**

CHOCOLATE-PEPPERMINT REFRIGERATOR COOKIES

1½ cups powdered sugar

1 cup margarine or butter, softened

1 egg

2⅔ cups all-purpose flour

¼ teaspoon salt

¼ cup cocoa

1 tablespoon milk

¼ cup finely crushed peppermint candy

Mix powdered sugar, margarine and egg in large bowl. Stir in flour and salt. Divide dough in half. Stir cocoa and milk into one half and peppermint candy into other half.

Shape chocolate dough into rectangle, 12 × 6½ inches, on waxed paper. Shape peppermint dough into roll, 12 inches long; place on chocolate dough. Wrap chocolate dough around peppermint dough using waxed paper to help lift. Press edges together. Wrap and refrigerate about 2 hours or until firm.

Heat oven to 375°. Cut rolls into ¼-inch slices. Place about 1 inch apart on ungreased cookie sheet. Bake 8 to 10 minutes or until set. Remove from cookie sheet. **4 dozen cookies.**

Chocolate-Wintergreen Refrigerator Cookies: Omit peppermint candies. Stir ¼ cup chocolate shot, ¼ teaspoon wintergreen extract and 4 drops green food color into plain dough. Continue as directed.

Maple-Nut Refrigerator Cookies

Rum-Raisin Sandwich Cookies

1 cup powdered sugar

1 cup margarine or butter, softened

1 egg

2¼ cups all-purpose flour

¼ teaspoon cream of tartar

1 cup raisins, finely chopped

Rum Filling (below)

Mix powdered sugar, margarine and egg in large bowl. Stir in remaining ingredients except Rum Filling. Divide dough in half. Shape each half into roll, 10 inches long. Wrap and refrigerate about 2 hours or until firm.

Heat oven to 375°. Cut rolls into ¼-inch slices; gently reshape slices into circles if necessary. Place about 1 inch apart on ungreased cookie sheet. Bake 7 to 9 minutes or until set. Remove from cookie sheet. Cool completely. Prepare Rum Filling. Put cookies together in pairs with about 1 teaspoon filling each. **About 3 dozen sandwich cookies.**

Rum Filling

2 cups powdered sugar

¼ cup margarine or butter, softened

2 tablespoons milk

¼ teaspoon rum extract

Mix all ingredients until smooth.

RUSSIAN TEACAKES

Macadamia nuts make these rich little cookies even richer.

1 cup margarine or butter, softened

½ cup powdered sugar

1 teaspoon vanilla

2¼ cups all-purpose flour

¾ cup finely chopped nuts

¼ teaspoon salt

Powdered sugar

Heat oven to 400°. Mix margarine, ½ cup powdered sugar and the vanilla in large bowl. Stir in flour, nuts and salt.

Shape dough into 1-inch balls. Place about 2 inches apart on ungreased cookie sheet. Bake 8 to 9 minutes or until set but not brown. Immediately remove from cookie sheet; roll in powdered sugar. Cool completely. Roll in powdered sugar. **About 4 dozen cookies.**

BUTTERSCOTCH-OATMEAL CRINKLES

2 cups packed brown sugar

½ cup margarine or butter

½ cup shortening

1 teaspoon vanilla

2 eggs

2¼ cups all-purpose flour

2 cups quick-cooking oats

1½ teaspoons baking powder

½ teaspoon salt

½ cup granulated or powdered sugar

Heat oven to 350°. Grease cookie sheet. Mix brown sugar, margarine, shortening, vanilla and eggs in large bowl. Stir in remaining ingredients except granulated sugar.

Shape dough into 1-inch balls; roll in granulated sugar. Place about 2 inches apart on cookie sheet. Bake 10 to 12 minutes or until almost no indentation remains when touched lightly in center. Immediately remove from cookie sheet. **About 5 dozen cookies.**

Molded Cookie

LEMON-ROSEMARY SLICES

Here is a distinctive combination of flavors, light and fragrant.

1 cup sugar

1 cup margarine or butter, softened

1 tablespoon grated lemon peel

1 teaspoon finely chopped fresh rosemary
   or ¼ teaspoon crushed, dried rosemary

2 eggs

3 cups all-purpose flour

½ teaspoon baking soda

¼ teaspoon salt

3 tablespoons sugar

1 teaspoon grated lemon peel

Mix 1 cup sugar, the margarine, 1 tablespoon lemon peel, the rosemary and eggs in large bowl. Stir in flour, baking soda and salt. Shape dough into roll, 12 inches long. Wrap and refrigerate about 2 hours or until firm.

Heat oven to 375°. Mix 3 tablespoons of sugar and 1 teaspoon lemon peel. Roll dough in sugar mixture to coat. Cut into ¼-inch slices. Place about 2 inches apart on ungreased cookie sheet. Bake 10 to 12 minutes or until edges are light brown. Immediately remove from cookie sheet. **About 4 dozen cookies.**

Lemon-Rosemary Slices

SNICKERDOODLES

For hundreds of years these cinnamon-sugar cookies have been known by their amusing name.

¼ cup sugar	2 eggs
1 tablespoon ground cinnamon	2¾ cups all-purpose flour
1½ cups sugar	2 teaspoons cream of tartar
½ cup shortening	1 teaspoon baking soda
½ cup margarine or butter, softened	¼ teaspoon salt

Heat oven to 400°. Mix ¼ cup sugar and the cinnamon; reserve. Mix 1½ cups sugar, the shortening, margarine and eggs in large bowl. Stir in flour, cream of tartar, baking soda and salt.

Shape dough into 1¼-inch balls. Roll in sugar mixture to coat. Place about 2 inches apart on ungreased cookie sheet. Bake about 10 minutes or until center is almost set. Remove from cookie sheet. **About 4 dozen cookies.**

THREE-LEAF CLOVERS

1 cup margarine or butter, softened	2⅓ cups all-purpose flour
⅓ cup sugar	½ teaspoon ground cloves
2 tablespoons honey	2 tablespoons sugar
1 egg	¼ teaspoon ground cloves

Heat oven to 350°. Mix margarine, ⅓ cup sugar, the honey and egg in large bowl. Stir in flour and ½ teaspoon cloves.

Shape dough into ¾-inch balls. Place 3 balls of dough together in a triangle. Place triangles about 2 inches apart on ungreased cookie sheet. Mix 2 tablespoons sugar and ¼ teaspoon cloves. Flatten cookies to about ¼ inch with greased bottom of glass dipped in sugar mixture. Bake 10 to 12 minutes or until edges are light brown. Remove from cookie sheet. **About 2 dozen cookies.**

Snickerdoodles, Three-leaf Clovers

Molded Cookie

ALMOND BONBONS

In the place of almond paste, try wrapping this dough around nuts, chocolate chunks or dried fruit. Tint the glaze for a more festive look and decorate as desired.

1½ cups all-purpose flour

½ cup margarine or butter, softened

⅓ cup powdered sugar

2 tablespoons milk

½ teaspoon vanilla

1 package (3½ ounces) almond paste

Glaze (below)

Sliced almonds, toasted if desired

Heat oven to 375°. Mix flour, margarine, powdered sugar, milk and vanilla in large bowl. Cut almond paste into ½-inch slices; cut each slice into fourths.

Shape 1-inch ball of dough around each piece of almond paste. Gently roll to form ball. Place about 1 inch apart on ungreased cookie sheet. Bake 10 to 12 minutes or until set and bottom is golden brown. Remove from cookie sheet. Cool completely. Prepare Glaze and dip in tops of cookies. Garnish with sliced almonds. **About 3 dozen cookies.**

GLAZE

1 cup powdered sugar

4 to 5 teaspoons milk

½ teaspoon almond extract

Mix all ingredients until smooth and desired consistency.

Almond Bonbons

THUMBPRINT COOKIES

Chocolate baking pieces, gumdrops and frostings are all delicious alternatives to jam for filling the thumbprint.

¼ cup packed brown sugar

¼ cup shortening

¼ cup margarine or butter, softened

½ teaspoon vanilla

1 egg yolk

1 cup all-purpose flour

¼ teaspoon salt

1 egg white

1 cup finely chopped nuts

About ½ cup jam or jelly (any flavor)

Heat oven to 350°. Mix brown sugar, shortening, margarine, vanilla and egg yolk in large bowl. Stir in flour and salt.

Shape dough into 1-inch balls. Beat egg white slightly with fork. Dip each ball into egg white; roll in nuts. Place about 1 inch apart on ungreased cookie sheet. Press thumb deeply in center of each. Bake about 10 minutes or until light brown. Quickly remake thumbprints with end of wooden spoon if necessary. Remove cookies from cookie sheet. Fill thumbprints with jam while cookies are warm. **About 2½ dozen cookies.**

PEANUT BUTTER COOKIES

½ cup granulated sugar

½ cup packed brown sugar

½ cup peanut butter

¼ cup shortening

¼ cup margarine or butter, softened

1 egg

1¼ cups all-purpose flour

¾ teaspoon baking soda

½ teaspoon baking powder

¼ teaspoon salt

Granulated sugar

Mix sugars, peanut butter, shortening, margarine and egg in large bowl. Stir in remaining ingredients except granulated sugar. Cover and refrigerate about 2 hours or until firm.

Heat oven to 375°. Shape dough into 1¼-inch balls. Place about 3 inches apart on ungreased cookie sheet. Flatten in crisscross pattern with greased fork dipped in sugar. Bake 9 to 10 minutes or until light brown. Cool 5 minutes; remove from cookie sheet. **About 2½ dozen cookies.**

Thumbprint Cookies, Black-eyed Susans (page 96)

CHEWY GINGER COOKIES

Fresh gingerroot gives a real kick to these chewy cookies. For a crisper cookie, bake two to three minutes longer.

1 cup sugar	1 tablespoon ground ginger
¾ cup margarine or butter	1 tablespoon finely chopped fresh gingerroot
¼ cup molasses	2 teaspoons baking soda
1 egg	¼ teaspoon salt
2⅓ cups all-purpose flour	Sugar

Heat oven to 375°. Mix sugar, margarine, molasses and egg in large bowl. Stir in remaining ingredients except sugar.

Shape dough into 1-inch balls. Roll in sugar. Place about 2 inches apart on ungreased cookie sheet; flatten slightly. Bake 7 to 9 minutes or until edges are set. Remove from cookie sheet. **About 4½ dozen cookies.**

HONEY-OAT SANDWICH COOKIES

For soft cookies, let the filled cookies stand overnight; for crisp cookies, fill just before serving.

1 cup packed brown sugar	1½ cups all-purpose flour
½ cup margarine or butter, softened	1½ cups quick-cooking or old-fashioned oats
½ cup shortening	
⅓ cup honey	2 teaspoons baking soda
2 eggs	Granulated sugar
1 teaspoon vanilla	About 1 cup thick fruit preserves (any flavor)

Heat oven to 350°. Mix brown sugar, margarine, shortening, honey, eggs and vanilla in large bowl. Stir in flour, oats and baking soda.

Shape dough into 1¼-inch balls. Place about 2 inches apart on ungreased cookie sheet. Flatten slightly with greased bottom of glass dipped in granulated sugar. Bake 8 to 10 minutes or until almost no indentation remains when touched lightly in center. Remove from cookie sheet. Cool completely. Put cookies together in pairs with about 1½ teaspoons preserves each. **About 3 dozen sandwich cookies.**

MERINGUE-TOPPED ALMOND COOKIES

2 egg whites

¼ teaspoon cream of tartar

½ cup granulated sugar

1 can (8 ounces) almond paste

½ cup margarine or butter, softened

1 cup packed brown sugar

1 teaspoon vanilla

2 egg yolks

1½ cups all-purpose flour

Granulated sugar

About 3 dozen whole almonds

Heat oven to 350°. Beat egg whites and cream of tartar in medium bowl on high speed until foamy. Beat in granulated sugar, 1 tablespoon at a time. Continue beating until stiff and glossy; reserve. Crumble almond paste into large bowl. Beat in margarine on medium speed until smooth. Stir in brown sugar, vanilla and egg yolks. Stir in flour.

Shape dough into 1¼-inch balls. Place about 2 inches apart on ungreased cookie sheet. Flatten slightly with greased bottom of glass dipped in granulated sugar. Spread about 1 rounded teaspoonful meringue on each cookie and top with almond. Bake 13 to 15 minutes or until meringue is golden brown. Remove from cookie sheet. **About 3 dozen cookies.**

BANANA-CORNMEAL COOKIES

¼ cup granulated sugar

½ teaspoon ground cinnamon

1 cup packed brown sugar

½ cup granulated sugar

½ cup margarine or butter, softened

½ cup mashed ripe banana (1 large)

1 egg

2½ cups all-purpose flour

1 cup yellow cornmeal

1 teaspoon baking powder

½ teaspoon salt

1 teaspoon ground cinnamon

Heat oven to 375°. Grease cookie sheet. Mix ¼ cup granulated sugar and ½ teaspoon cinnamon; reserve. Mix brown sugar, ½ cup granulated sugar, the margarine, banana and egg in large bowl. Stir in flour, cornmeal, baking powder, salt and 1 teaspoon cinnamon. (If dough is too soft to shape, cover and refrigerate about 2 hours or until firm.)

Shape dough into 1¼-inch balls. Place about 3 inches apart on cookie sheet. Flatten in crisscross pattern with greased fork dipped in reserved sugar mixture. Bake 10 to 12 minutes or until light brown. Immediately remove from cookie sheet. **About 4 dozen cookies.**

Molded Cookie

Lemon Decorator Cookies

Make your own cookie presses out of carrots, following the designs here or designs of your own. Regular cookie presses work well too, of course.

1 cup margarine or butter, softened

1 package (3 ounces) cream cheese, softened

½ cup sugar

1 tablespoon grated lemon peel

2 cups all-purpose flour

Carrot Press (below)

Sugar

Mix margarine and cream cheese in large bowl. Stir in sugar and lemon peel. Gradually stir in flour. Cover and refrigerate about 2 hours or until firm. Carve Carrot Press.

Heat oven to 375°. Shape dough into 1-inch balls. Place about 2 inches apart on ungreased cookie sheet. Flatten to about ¼ inch with Carrot Press dipped in sugar. Bake 7 to 9 minutes or until set but not brown. Remove from cookie sheet. **About 5 dozen cookies.**

Carrot Press: *Cut about 1½-inch diameter carrot into 2-inch lengths. Cut decorative design about ⅛ inch deep in cut end of carrot. Use small, sharp knife, tip of vegetable peeler or other small, sharp kitchen tool to make designs.*

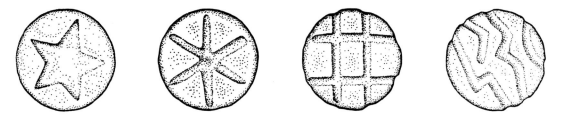

Cut decorative designs about ⅛ inch deep in ends of carrot pieces.

Lemon Decorator Cookies

BLACK-EYED SUSANS

¾ cup margarine or butter, softened

½ cup sugar

1 teaspoon vanilla

12 drops yellow food color

1 egg

1 package (3 ounces) cream cheese, softened

2 cups all-purpose flour

About 3 dozen chocolate deluxe baking pieces

Mix margarine, sugar, vanilla, food color, egg and cream cheese in large bowl. Stir in flour. Cover and refrigerate dough about 2 hours or until firm.

Heat oven to 375°. Shape dough into 1¼-inch balls. Place about 2 inches apart on ungreased cookie sheet. Using scissors, cut from top into 6 wedges about three-fourths way through dough. Spread wedges apart slightly. (Cookies will flatten as they bake.) Bake 10 to 12 minutes or until set and edges begin to brown. Immediately press baking piece in center of each cookie. Remove from cookie sheet. **About 3 dozen cookies.**

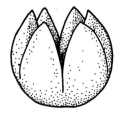

Cut balls from top into 6 wedges about ¾ way through dough.

ANIMAL COOKIES

These cookies are a terrific solution to rainy-day blues. If the dough softens too much, cover and refrigerate until firm (about one hour).

½ cup granulated sugar

½ cup packed brown sugar

½ cup margarine or butter, softened

1 teaspoon vanilla

1 egg

2 cups all-purpose flour

1 teaspoon baking powder

½ teaspoon salt

½ teaspoon ground cinnamon

Heat oven to 350°. Mix sugars, margarine, vanilla and egg in large bowl. Stir in remaining ingredients. (If dough is too soft to shape, cover and refrigerate about 2 hours or until firm.)

Shape dough 2 tablespoons at a time into slightly flattened balls and ropes. Arrange on ungreased cookie sheet to form animals as desired. Bake about 10 to 12 minutes or until edges are golden brown. **About 1½ dozen cookies.**

Letter and Number Cookies: Prepare dough as directed. Shape level tablespoonfuls dough into ropes, about 8 inches long and about ¼ inch thick. Shape into letters and numbers as desired on ungreased cookie sheet. Bake 8 to 10 minutes. Cool 3 minutes; remove from cookie sheet. **About 3 dozen cookies.**

Arrange balls or ropes of dough on cookie sheet to form animals as desired.

Molded Cookie

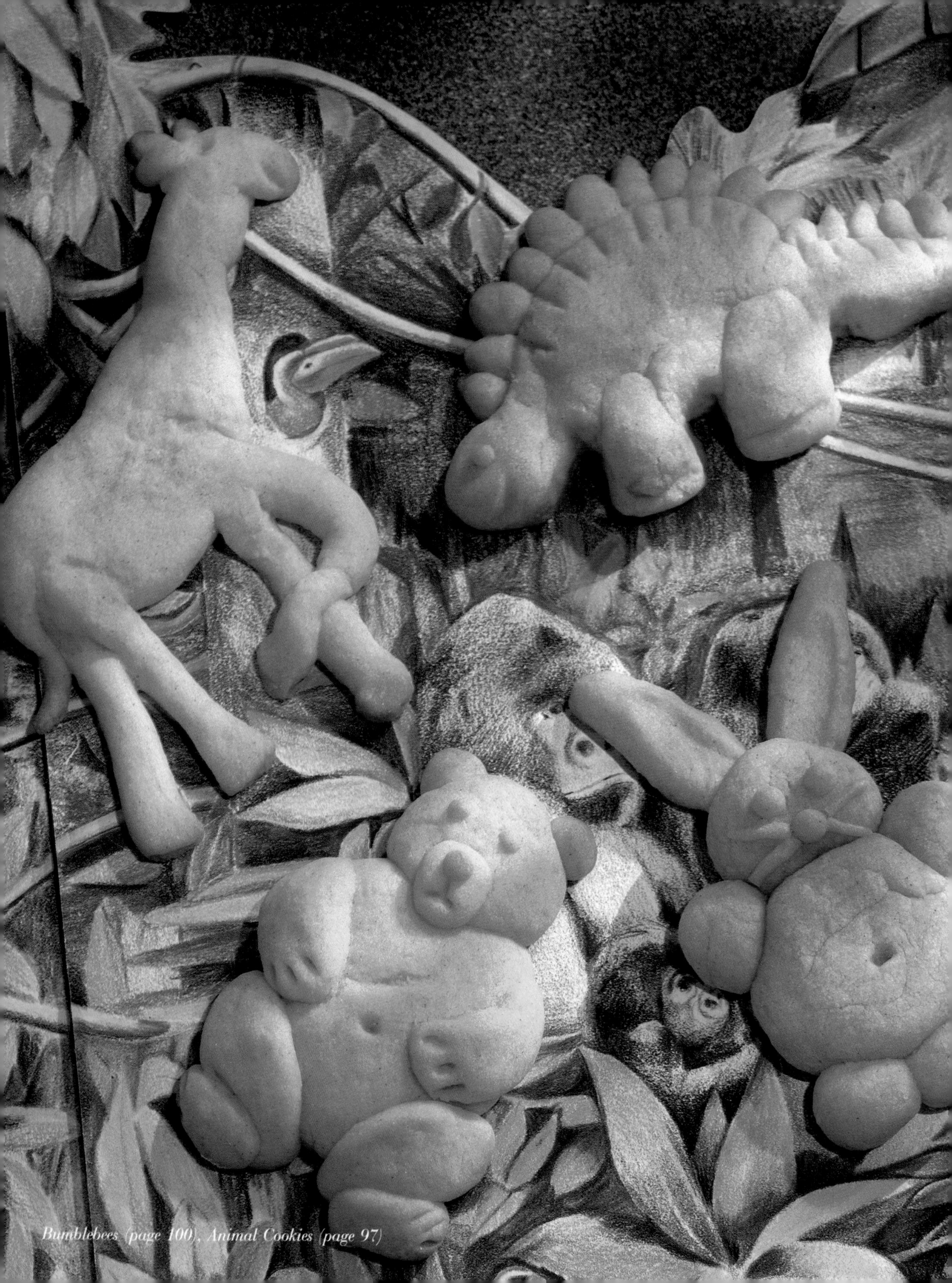

Bumblebees (page 100), Animal Cookies (page 97)

BUMBLEBEES

½ cup peanut butter

⅓ cup packed brown sugar

⅓ cup honey

½ cup shortening

1 egg

1¾ cups all-purpose flour

¾ teaspoon baking soda

½ teaspoon baking powder

About 8 dozen small pretzel twists

About 8 dozen small pretzel sticks

Mix peanut butter, brown sugar, honey, shortening and egg in large bowl. Stir in flour, baking soda and baking powder. Cover and refrigerate about 2 hours or until firm.

Heat oven to 350°. Shape dough into 1-inch balls. (Dough will be slightly sticky.) Arrange 2 pretzel twists side by side, rounded sides together, on ungreased cookie sheet. Place 1 ball of dough on center of pretzels; flatten dough slightly. Break 2 pretzel sticks in half. Gently press 3 pieces into dough for stripes on bee.

Break remaining piece in half. Insert in 1 end of dough for antennae. Repeat with remaining dough and pretzels. Bake 11 to 13 minutes or until light golden brown. Remove from cookie sheet. **About 4 dozen cookies.**

CINNAMON TWISTS

1 cup sugar

½ cup margarine or butter, softened

2 teaspoons vanilla

1 egg

1¾ cups all-purpose flour

2 teaspoons baking powder

½ teaspoon salt

1 teaspoon ground cinnamon

Heat oven to 375°. Mix sugar, margarine, vanilla and egg in large bowl. Stir in flour, baking powder and salt. Divide dough in half; stir cinnamon into one half.

Shape 1 level teaspoonful dough from each half into 3-inch rope. Place ropes side by side; twist gently. Repeat with remaining dough. Place twists about 2 inches apart on ungreased cookie sheet. Bake 8 to 10 minutes or until very light brown. Remove from cookie sheet. **About 4 dozen cookies.**

KRINGLA

1½ cups sugar

1 egg

2½ cups sour cream

4 cups all-purpose flour

2 teaspoons baking soda

¼ teaspoon salt

Heat oven to 350°. Mix sugar, egg and sour cream in large bowl. Stir in flour, baking soda and salt.

Spoon dough by rounded teaspoonfuls onto floured surface; roll in flour to coat. Roll into rope, 7 to 8 inches long. Form each rope into figure 8, tucking ends under, on ungreased cookie sheet. Bake 12 to 15 minutes or until light golden brown. Immediately remove from cookie sheet. **About 6 dozen cookies.**

Molded Cookie

CHOCOLATE-DIPPED ORANGE PRETZELS

Orange and walnut are flavors typical of Greek sweets. This cookie is similar to the Greek **koulourakia**, *traditionally shaped into rings, the figure 8 and Greek letters.*

½ cup sugar

½ cup grated orange peel

¼ cup ground walnuts

½ cup margarine or butter

2 eggs

2 cups all-purpose flour

1 tablespoon orange juice

1 teaspoon baking powder

¼ teaspoon ground cinnamon

¾ cup semisweet chocolate chips, melted

Heat oven to 350°. Grease cookie sheet. Process sugar and orange peel in food processor until finely ground. Stir in walnuts. Beat margarine and eggs in large bowl until smooth. Stir in sugar mixture and remaining ingredients except melted chocolate until well blended.

Shape 1-inch balls of dough into 10-inch ropes. Twist each rope into pretzel shape on cookie sheet. Bake 10 to 12 minutes or until edges are light brown. Remove from cookie sheet. Cool completely. Dip tops of pretzels in melted chocolate. Place on waxed paper until chocolate is set. **About 2 dozen pretzels.**

CHOCOLATE-BOURBON BALLS

2 cups finely crushed chocolate wafer crumbs
  (about 38 cookies)

2 cups finely chopped almonds

2 cups powdered sugar

½ cup bourbon

¼ cup light corn syrup

Powdered sugar

Mix wafer crumbs, almonds and 2 cups powdered sugar in large bowl. Stir in bourbon and corn syrup.

Shape mixture into 1-inch balls. Roll in powdered sugar. Cover tightly and refrigerate at least 5 days to blend flavors. **About 5 dozen cookies.**

Chocolate-dipped Orange Pretzels, Chocolate-Bourbon Balls

NO-BAKE APRICOT BALLS

These easy treats are delicious when eaten right away, but they're even better after a day or two when the flavors have had a chance to blend.

1 package (8 ounces) dried apricots

1 cup hazelnuts

2 cups graham cracker crumbs

1 can (12 ounces) sweetened condensed milk

Place apricots and hazelnuts in food processor. Cover and process, using quick on-and-off motions, until finely chopped. Place mixture in large bowl. Stir in graham cracker crumbs and milk.

Shape dough into 1-inch balls. If desired, press whole hazelnut into each ball. Cover tightly and store in refrigerator up to 2 weeks or freeze up to 2 months. **About 7½ dozen cookies.**

No-bake Apple Balls: Substitute dried apples for the apricots and walnuts for the hazelnuts.

QUICK PEANUT BUTTER AND JAM STICKS

½ cup granulated sugar

½ cup packed brown sugar

½ cup shortening

½ cup peanut butter

1 egg

1½ cups all-purpose flour

1 teaspoon baking powder

¼ teaspoon salt

¼ cup strawberry jam

Glaze (below)

Heat oven to 375°. Mix sugars, shortening, peanut butter and egg in large bowl. Stir in flour, baking powder and salt.

Divide dough into fourths. Shape each fourth into rectangle, 10 × 1½ inches, on ungreased cookie sheet. Make indentation lengthwise down center of each rectangle with wooden spoon handle. Fill each with 1 tablespoon jam. Bake 10 to 12 minutes or until golden brown. Cool 5 minutes. Prepare Glaze. Cut each rectangle crosswise into 1-inch slices. Drizzle with Glaze. Remove from cookie sheet. **About 3½ dozen cookies.**

GLAZE

1 cup powdered sugar

4 to 5 teaspoons milk

½ teaspoon vanilla

Mix all ingredients until smooth and desired consistency.

COCONUT-FUDGE CUPS

¼ cup margarine or butter, softened

1 package (3 ounces) cream cheese, softened

¾ cup all-purpose flour

¼ cup powdered sugar

2 tablespoons cocoa

½ teaspoon vanilla

Coconut-Fudge Filling (below)

Heat oven to 350°. Mix margarine and cream cheese in large bowl. Stir in remaining ingredients except Coconut Fudge Filling.

Pat 1-inch ball of dough in bottom and up side of each of 24 small ungreased muffin cups, 1¾ × 1 inch. Prepare Coconut Fudge Filling. Spoon about 2 teaspoons filling into each cup. Bake 18 to 20 minutes or until almost no indentation remains when filling is touched lightly. Cool slightly. Carefully remove from muffin cups. **2 dozen cookies.**

COCONUT-FUDGE FILLING

⅔ cup sugar

⅔ cup flaked coconut

⅓ cup cocoa

2 tablespoons margarine or butter, softened

1 egg

Mix all ingredients.

Ginger Shortbread Wedges

These are wonderful with "a spot of tea." Drop a piece of crystallized ginger in your teacup for an added treat.

⅔ cup margarine or butter, softened

⅓ cup powdered sugar

3 tablespoons finely chopped crystallized ginger

1⅓ cups all-purpose flour

2 teaspoons granulated sugar

Heat oven to 350°. Mix margarine, powdered sugar and ginger in large bowl. Stir in flour. Press dough into ungreased tart pan, 9 × 1 inch. Sprinkle with granulated sugar. Bake about 20 minutes or until golden brown. Cool 10 minutes; remove side of pan. Cut into wedges. **16 cookies.**

Fig-Filled—Whole Wheat Cookies

Fig Filling (below)

1 cup packed brown sugar

½ cup shortening

1 egg

1 teaspoon vanilla

1⅔ cups whole wheat flour

¼ teaspoon salt

Prepare Fig Filling. Heat oven to 375°. Mix brown sugar, shortening, egg and vanilla in large bowl. Stir in flour and salt.

Divide dough into thirds. Pat each third into rectangle, 12 × 4 inches, on waxed paper. Spoon one-third of filling lengthwise down center of dough in strip, 1½ inches wide. Fold sides of dough over filling, using waxed paper to help lift, and overlap edges slightly. Press lightly to seal. Cut into 1-inch bars. Place seam side down about 1 inch apart on ungreased cookie sheet. Repeat with remaining dough and filling. Bake 12 to 14 minutes or until light brown. Remove from cookie sheet. **About 3 dozen cookies.**

Fig Filling

1⅓ cups finely chopped dried figs

⅓ cup water

⅓ cup finely chopped nuts

¼ cup sugar

1 teaspoon grated orange peel

Heat all ingredients over medium heat about 5 minutes, stirring frequently, until thickened.

Apricot Bars: Substitute 1⅓ cups finely chopped dried apricots for the figs.

GIANT GINGER COOKIE

The directions below explain how to make a giant cookie clock. For variety, try a jack-o'-lantern, ladybug, face or anything else you like. A garlic press or potato ricer is very handy for making dough into "hair."

1 cup sugar

½ cup margarine or butter, softened

¼ cup molasses

1 egg

2 cups all-purpose flour

1½ teaspoons baking soda

½ teaspoon salt

½ teaspoon ground cinnamon

½ teaspoon ground ginger

¼ teaspoon ground cloves

Sugar

Heat oven to 375°. Grease 12-inch pizza pan or large cookie sheet. Mix 1 cup sugar, the margarine, molasses and egg in large bowl. Stir in flour, baking soda, salt, cinnamon, ginger and cloves.

Reserve ⅓ cup dough. Press remaining dough into pan or into 12-inch circle on cookie sheet. Shape reserved dough into numbers and arrows; place on dough in pan to resemble the face of a clock. Sprinkle with sugar. Bake about 10 minutes or until golden brown. Cool completely. Cut or break into pieces. **About 3½ dozen 1½-inch pieces.**

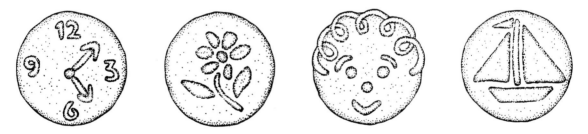

Shape reserved dough into desired design and place on dough in pan.

Molded Cookie

PISTACHIO-CHOCOLATE CHECKERS

1½ cups powdered sugar

1 cup margarine or butter, softened

1 egg

2⅔ cups all-purpose flour

¼ teaspoon salt

¼ cup cocoa

1 tablespoon milk

¼ cup finely chopped pistachios

2 or 3 drops green food color, if desired

Mix powdered sugar, margarine and egg in large bowl. Stir in flour and salt. Divide dough in half. Stir cocoa and milk into one half and pistachios and food color into other half.

Pat chocolate dough into rectangle, 6 × 5 inches. Cut crosswise into 8 strips, ¾ inch wide. Repeat with pistachio dough. Place 2 strips of each color of dough side by side, alternating colors. Top with 2 strips of each dough, alternating colors to create checkerboard. Gently press strips together. Repeat with remaining strips for second log. Wrap and refrigerate about 2 hours or until firm.

Heat oven to 375°. Cut rectangles crosswise into ¼-inch slices. Place about 1 inch apart on ungreased cookie sheet. Bake 8 to 10 minutes or until set. Remove from cookie sheet. **About 6 dozen cookies.**

SUNFLOWER COOKIES

1 cup sugar

½ cup margarine or butter, softened

1 teaspoon vanilla

1 egg

1⅓ cups all-purpose flour

1 cup quick-cooking oats

½ teaspoon baking powder

¼ teaspoon salt

½ cup unsalted sunflower nuts

¼ teaspoon yellow food color

Mix sugar, margarine, vanilla and egg in large bowl. Stir in flour, oats, baking powder and salt. Divide dough into one-third and two-thirds portions. Stir sunflower nuts into one-third dough and food color into two-thirds dough.

Shape sunflower nut dough into two ¾-inch rolls, 8 inches long. Divide yellow dough in half. Pat each half into rectangle, 8 × 4 inches, on floured surface. Wrap around 1 sunflower nut roll; repeat with remaining dough. Wrap and refrigerate about 2 hours or until firm.

Heat oven to 350°. Grease cookie sheet. Cut rolls into ¼-inch slices. Place about 2 inches apart on cookie sheet. Cut slits in outer yellow edge about every ½ inch to shape tips of petals. Bake 8 to 10 minutes or until light brown. Remove from cookie sheet. **About 4 dozen cookies.**

Pistachio-Chocolate Checkers, Sunflower Cookies, Coconut-Fudge Cups (page 105)

Molded Cookie

CHAPTER SIX
SPECIALTY COOKIES

▀▄▀▄▀▄▀▄▀▄▀▄▀▄▀▄▀▄▀▄▀▄▀▄▀▄▀▄▀▄▀▄

These cookies boast a little extra effort, either in their appearance or flavor. A "specialty" cookie may use a particular piece of bakeware or equipment to give the cookies their distinctive shape, such as the classically formed spritz cookie (below), which uses a cookie press. Another sort of specialty cookie is one traditional to the cooking of a particular country, as in the case of Italian biscotti (page 117), or one that calls for an unusual ingredient, such as Essence-of-Rose Cookies, (page 116). We think these cookies make an extra-special treat for friends and family.

▀▄▀▄▀▄▀▄▀▄▀▄▀▄▀▄▀▄▀▄▀▄▀▄▀▄▀▄▀▄▀▄

THE ULTIMATE
SPRITZ

1 cup margarine or butter, softened

½ cup sugar

2¼ cups all-purpose flour

¼ teaspoon salt

1 egg

¼ teaspoon almond extract or vanilla

Heat oven to 400°. Mix margarine and sugar in large bowl. Stir in remaining ingredients. Place dough in cookie press. Form desired shapes on ungreased cookie sheet. Decorate with currants, raisins, candies, colored sugar, finely chopped nuts or candied fruit or fruit peel, if desired. Bake 5 to 8 minutes or until set but not brown. Immediately remove from cookie sheet. To decorate cookies after baking, use a drop of corn syrup to attach decorations to cooled cookies. **6 to 7 dozen cookies.**

▀▄▀▄▀▄▀▄▀▄▀▄▀▄▀▄▀▄▀▄▀▄▀▄▀▄▀▄▀▄▀▄

The Ultimate Spritz, Date-filled Spritz (pages 112–113), Lime Meltaways (page 113)

HOLIDAY SPRITZ

1 cup margarine or butter, softened

½ cup sugar

2¼ cups all-purpose flour

¼ teaspoon salt

1 egg

1 teaspoon rum flavoring

Red or green food color

Butter Rum Glaze (below)

Heat oven to 400°. Mix margarine and sugar in large bowl. Stir in remaining ingredients except Butter Rum Glaze. Place dough in cookie press. Form desired shapes on ungreased cookie sheet. Bake 5 to 8 minutes or until set but not brown. Immediately remove from cookie sheet. Cool completely. Spread with glaze. **6 to 7 dozen cookies.**

BUTTER RUM GLAZE

¼ cup butter or margarine

1 cup powdered sugar

1 teaspoon rum flavoring

1 to 2 tablespoons hot water

Red or green food color, if desired

Heat butter in 1-quart saucepan over low heat until melted; remove from heat. Stir in powdered sugar and rum flavoring. Stir in hot water until glaze is of spreading consistency. Tint glaze with food color to match cookies if desired.

Chocolate Spritz: Stir 2 ounces unsweetened chocolate, melted and cooled, into the margarine-sugar mixture. Substitute almond extract or vanilla for the rum flavoring.

Spice Spritz: Stir in 1 teaspoon ground cinnamon, ½ teaspoon ground nutmeg and ¼ teaspoon ground allspice with the flour. Substitute vanilla for the rum flavoring.

DATE-FILLED SPRITZ

The Ultimate Spritz (page 111)

1 cup walnut pieces (about 4 ounces)

¼ cup sugar

¼ cup honey

2 tablespoons orange juice

1 teaspoon grated orange peel

1 box (8 ounces) pitted dates (about 1¼ cups)

Heat oven to 375°. Prepare spritz dough using vanilla. Place remaining ingredients in food processor. Cover and process about 20 seconds or to a thick paste.

Place dough in cookie press with ribbon tip. Form 10-inch ribbons about 2 inches apart on ungreased cookie sheet. Spoon filling down center of each ribbon to form ½-inch-wide strip.

Top each ribbon of dough and filling with another ribbon of dough. Gently press edges with fork to seal. Bake 12 to 15 minutes or until light brown. Immediately cut ribbons into 2-inch lengths. Remove from cookie sheet. **About 4 dozen cookies.**

LIME MELTAWAYS

These cookies are a refreshing dessert on summer days. They really do melt in your mouth.

1 cup margarine or butter

½ cup powdered sugar

1¾ cups all-purpose flour

¼ cup cornstarch

1 tablespoon grated lime peel

½ teaspoon vanilla

Lime Glaze (below)

Heat oven to 350°. Beat margarine and powdered sugar in large bowl until light and fluffy. Stir in remaining ingredients except Lime Glaze until well blended. Place dough in cookie press with ribbon tip. Form long ribbons of dough on ungreased cookie sheet. Cut into 3-inch lengths. Bake 9 to 11 minutes or until edges are golden brown. Remove from cookie sheet. Cool completely. Prepare Lime Glaze and brush on cookies. **About 4 dozen cookies.**

LIME GLAZE

½ cup powdered sugar

4 teaspoons lime juice

2 teaspoons grated lime peel

Mix all ingredients.

LADYFINGERS

Homemade ladyfingers are a treat, delicate and fresh. They are essential to Charlotte Russe and trifle.

3 eggs, separated	3 tablespoons water
¼ teaspoon cream of tartar	½ teaspoon vanilla
¼ cup sugar	¼ teaspoon baking powder
⅓ cup sugar	¼ teaspoon lemon extract, if desired
¾ cup all-purpose flour	⅛ teaspoon salt

Heat oven to 350°. Grease and flour cookie sheet. Beat egg whites and cream of tartar in large bowl until foamy. Gradually beat in ¼ cup sugar until stiff peaks form. Beat egg yolks and ⅓ cup sugar in medium bowl about 3 minutes or until thick and lemon colored. Stir in remaining ingredients. Fold egg yolk mixture into egg white mixture.

Place batter in decorating bag with #9 tip or cookie press with #32 tip. Form 3-inch fingers about 2 inches apart on cookie sheet. Bake 10 to 12 minutes or until set and light brown. Immediately remove from cookie sheet. Dust tops with powdered sugar. **About 3½ dozen cookies.**

ALMOND MACAROONS

1 can (8 ounces) almond paste	¼ teaspoon almond extract
¼ cup all-purpose flour	2 egg whites
1¼ cups powdered sugar	3 dozen blanched whole almonds

Grease cookie sheet. Mix almond paste, flour, powdered sugar, almond extract and egg whites in large bowl. Beat on medium speed 2 minutes, scraping bowl occasionally, until smooth.

Place dough in decorating bag fitted with #9 rosette tip. Pipe 1½-inch cookies about 2 inches apart on cookie sheet. Top each with whole almond. Refrigerate 30 minutes. Heat oven to 325°. Bake about 12 minutes or until edges are light brown. Immediately remove from cookie sheet. Cool completely. Store in airtight container. **About 3 dozen cookies.**

Ladyfingers, Almond Macaroons

SWEDISH HALF-MOON COOKIES

This tender cookie is made with potato flour (sometimes called "potato starch"). It is often found in stores near the cornstarch, in a section with gluten-free products and in health-food stores. The filling of cherry preserves is delightful with the almond-scented pastry.

1¾ cups all-purpose flour	1 egg
½ cup potato flour	½ cup cherry preserves
½ cup powdered sugar	1 egg white, beaten
1 cup margarine or butter, well chilled and cut into cubes	¼ cup sanding sugar
	¼ cup finely chopped blanched almonds
⅛ teaspoon almond extract	

Mix flours and powdered sugar in large bowl. Cut margarine into dry mixture using pastry blender until mixture resembles fine crumbs. Stir in almond extract and egg until dough leaves side of bowl. Cover and refrigerate 1 hour.

Heat oven to 350°. Line cookie sheet with cooking parchment paper. Roll one-fourth of dough at a time ⅛ inch thick between 2 sheets of waxed paper. (Keep remaining dough refrigerated until ready to roll.) Cut with fluted 3-inch round biscuit cutter. Spoon ½ teaspoon cherry preserves onto half of each cookie. Fold dough over preserves to form half-moon shape. Pinch edges to seal. Place on cookie sheet. Brush with egg white; sprinkle with sanding sugar and almonds. Bake 10 to 12 minutes or until edges are light brown. Remove from cookie sheet. **About 3 dozen cookies.**

ESSENCE-OF-ROSE COOKIES

For these little cookies, use flower-shaped cutters, canapé cutters or other small designs. Rose extract is available at specialty shops; almond extract is a nice substitute.

½ cup sugar	1¼ cups all-purpose flour
⅓ cup margarine or butter, softened	½ teaspoon baking powder
⅛ teaspoon rose extract	¼ teaspoon salt
2 drops red food color	Red or pink sugar
1 egg	

Mix sugar, margarine, rose extract, food color and egg in large bowl. Stir in flour, baking powder and salt. Cover and refrigerate 2 hours or until firm.

Heat oven to 350°. Roll half of dough at a time ⅛ inch thick on lightly floured surface. Cut into desired shapes with 1-inch cookie cutters. Place about 1 inch apart on ungreased cookie sheet. Sprinkle with colored sugar. Bake 6 to 8 minutes or until light brown on bottom. Remove from cookie sheet. **About 2 dozen cookies.**

ANISE BISCOTTI

Biscotti are cookies that have been baked twice—first as a loaf, then a second time sliced—until they are thoroughly dry and crisp.

1 cup sugar	2 eggs
½ cup margarine or butter, softened	3½ cups all-purpose flour
2 teaspoons anise seed, ground	1 teaspoon baking powder
2 teaspoons grated lemon peel	½ teaspoon salt

Heat oven to 350°. Beat sugar, margarine, anise seed, lemon peel and eggs in large bowl. Stir in flour, baking powder and salt.

Shape half of dough at a time into rectangle, 10 × 3 inches, on ungreased cookie sheet. Bake about 20 minutes or until toothpick inserted in center comes out clean. Cool on cookie sheet 15 minutes.

Cut crosswise into ½-inch slices. Place with cut sides down on cookie sheet. Bake about 15 minutes or until crisp and light brown. Remove from cookie sheet. **About 3½ dozen cookies.**

Orange Biscotti: Omit anise seed and lemon peel. Add 1 tablespoon grated orange peel to the margarine mixture.

PALMIERS

Palmiers ("palm leaves," in French) are very easy to make from commercial puff pastry. The dusting of granulated sugar caramelizes in the oven. To make sixty palmiers, use one whole package of puff pastry dough.

½ package (17¼-ounce size) frozen puff
    pastry dough

½ cup sugar

1 ounce semisweet chocolate, melted

Heat oven to 375°. Lightly grease cookie sheet. Roll dough into ⅛-inch-thick rectangle, 12 × 9½ inches, on sugared surface. Mark a line lengthwise down center of dough. Fold long sides toward center line, leaving ¼ inch at center. Fold dough in half lengthwise to form strip, 12 × 2½ inches, pressing dough together.

Cut dough strip crosswise into ¼-inch slices. Coat slices with sugar. Place about 2 inches apart on cookie sheet. Bake 8 to 10 minutes, turning after 5 minutes, until cookies begin to turn golden brown. Immediately remove from cookie sheet. Cool completely. Dip ends of cookies into melted chocolate. Place on waxed paper until chocolate is firm. **About 2½ dozen cookies.**

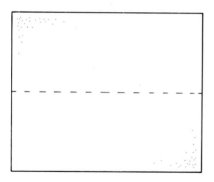

Mark a line lengthwise down center of dough.

Fold long sides toward center line, leaving ¼ inch at center.

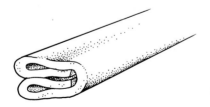

Fold dough in half lengthwise to form strip.

Cut dough strip crosswise into slices.

Anise Biscotti (page 117), Palmiers

GINGERBREAD COOKIE TREE

This "tree" is an edible centerpiece that can be made from stars, hearts, fluted circles or rings. Ten cutters, ranging from 2 to 8¾ inches (increasing by ¾ inch from one size to the next) are required. Nested cookie-cutter sets are available in specialty shops, but homemade patterns work just as well.

2 recipes Gingerbread Cookies (page 61)	**4 to 5 tablespoons half-and-half**
4 cups powdered sugar	**Assorted candies, if desired**
1 teaspoon vanilla	

Prepare and refrigerate recipes individually as directed. Heat oven to 350°. Lightly grease cookie sheet.

Roll half of 1 recipe of dough at a time ¼ inch thick on floured surface. Cut 3 cookies of each size with floured cutters or patterns. Place about 2 inches apart on cookie sheet. Bake large cookies 12 to 14 minutes and small cookies 8 to 10 minutes or until no indentation remains when touched. Cool slightly; remove from cookie sheet. Cool completely.

Beat powdered sugar, vanilla and half-and-half until smooth and spreading of consistency. Assemble tree on serving plate or foil-covered cardboard: Starting with largest cookies, stack cookies as frosted, or stack unfrosted cookies together with small dab of frosting in center of each. Let layers dry or hold cookies in place with bamboo skewers if necessary. Use remaining frosting to pipe "snow" on the tree with decorating bag. Decorate with assorted candies. **1 cookie tree.**

Gingerbread Cookie Tree

Springerle

From Germany comes this embossed Christmas cookie with centuries of tradition. A springerle rolling pin has recessed designs that make an imprint on the dough. The imprinted cookies are separated, then traditionally allowed to dry overnight, which helps set the design. We don't recommend air drying because the dough contains raw egg; if there isn't time to bake the cookies immediately, refrigerate (in a single layer, loosely covered) up to twenty-four hours. These richly flavored cookies are very hard—excellent for dunking.

1 cup sugar	2 cups all-purpose flour
2 eggs	2 teaspoons anise seed

Heat oven to 325°. Beat sugar and eggs in large bowl about 5 minutes or until thick and lemon colored. Stir in flour and anise seed.

Roll half of dough at a time ¼ inch thick on floured cloth-covered surface. Roll well-floured springerle rolling pin over dough to emboss with designs. Cut out cookies. Place about 1 inch apart on ungreased cookie sheet. Bake 12 to 15 minutes or until light brown. Immediately remove from cookie sheet. **About 3 dozen cookies.**

Pizzelles

These Italian cookies are wafer-thin and lightly flavored with anise. They are cooked in a hot pizzelle iron, also known as a cialde iron. If you work quickly, you can roll the hot cookie into a cylinder.

2 cups all-purpose flour	1 tablespoon anise extract or vanilla
1 cup sugar	4 eggs, slightly beaten
¾ cup margarine or butter, melted and cooled	

Preheat pizzelle iron according to manufacturers' directions. Mix flour, sugar, margarine, anise extract and eggs. Drop 1 tablespoon batter onto heated pizzelle iron; close. Cook about 30 seconds or until golden brown. Carefully remove pizzelle from iron. Cool on wire rack. Repeat for each cookie. **About 3½ dozen cookies.**

Bottom: Springerle, Middle: Krumkake (page 124), Top: Pizzelles

KRUMKAKE

Making these charming cookies takes a little practice. Be prepared to adjust the heat and cooking time to get the desired color. Each hot cookie wafer is quickly rolled around a cone-shaped mold. Using two molds is easier; if only one is available, remove it from the cooling cookie before the next cookie is done. Try serving krumkakes filled with whipped cream, lightly sweetened, or garnished with fruit.

1 cup sugar	2 teaspoons cornstarch
¾ cup all-purpose flour	1 teaspoon vanilla
½ cup margarine or butter, melted	4 eggs
⅓ cup whipping (heavy) cream	

Beat all ingredients until smooth. Heat krumkake iron over small electric or gas unit on medium-high heat until hot (grease iron lightly if necessary). Pour scant tablespoon batter on iron; close gently. Heat each side about 15 seconds or until light golden brown. Keep iron over heat at all times. Carefully remove cookie. Immediately roll around cone-shaped roller. Remove roller when cookie is set. **About 4 dozen cookies.**

ORANGE MADELEINES

Sponge cakes in miniature, French madeleines are baked in shell-shaped molds. If you must bake the recipe in two batches, don't let the batter sit any longer than it has to or the second batch will not be as tender as the first.

1 egg, separated	1 tablespoon orange-flavored liqueur or milk
½ cup sugar	1½ teaspoons baking powder
1 cup all-purpose flour	1½ teaspoons grated orange peel
½ cup milk	¼ teaspoon salt
2 tablespoons vegetable oil	Powdered sugar

Heat oven to 375°. Grease and flour twenty-four 3-inch* madeleine molds. Beat egg white in small bowl until foamy. Beat in ¼ cup of the sugar, 1 tablespoon at a time. Continue beating until very stiff and glossy. Set meringue aside. Beat remaining ¼ cup sugar with remaining ingredients except powdered sugar in medium bowl on high 2 minutes, scraping bowl occasionally. Fold in meringue.

Fill molds two-thirds full. Tap pan firmly on counter to remove air bubbles. Bake 10 to 12 minutes or until edges are light brown. Cool slightly; remove from pan. Sprinkle with powdered sugar just before serving. **About 2 dozen cookies.**

One 12-mold pan can be used. Bake half of batter; wash, grease and flour pan. Bake remaining batter.

COOKIE-MOLD COOKIES

Slightly spicy with a hint of almond, these cookies are reminiscent of the Dutch-heritage, store-bought cookies in the shape of windmills. If you have windmill molds, use them, but any cookie mold will do. Molds have been used to shape cookies in China and Europe for hundreds of years, and some American molds date to the eighteenth century.

¾ cup packed brown sugar

½ cup margarine or butter, softened

¼ cup molasses

½ teaspoon vanilla

1 egg

2¼ cups all-purpose flour

¾ cup coarsely chopped sliced almonds

½ teaspoon ground allspice

¼ teaspoon salt

¼ teaspoon baking soda

Mix brown sugar, margarine, molasses, vanilla and egg in large bowl. Stir in remaining ingredients. Cover and refrigerate 2 hours or until firm.

Heat oven to 350°. Lightly grease cookie sheet. Flour wooden or ceramic cookie mold(s). Tap mold to remove excess flour. Firmly press small amounts of dough into mold, adding more dough until mold is full and making sure dough is of uniform thickness across mold. Hold mold upside down and tap edge firmly several times on hard surface (such as a counter or cutting board). If cookie does not come out, turn mold and tap another edge until cookie comes out of mold. Place cookies on cookie sheet. Bake 8 to 10 minutes for 2-inch cookies, 10 to 12 minutes for 5-inch cookies or until edges are light brown. (Time depends on thickness of cookies. Watch carefully.) **About 4½ dozen 2-inch cookies or 2 dozen 5-inch cookies.**

Cast-Iron Cookie-Mold Directions: Grease and flour iron cookie mold(s). Press dough into mold as directed above. Bake smaller molds about 15 minutes, larger molds about 20 minutes. Cool cookies 10 minutes; remove from molds.

Orange Madeleines (page 124). Cookie-mold Cookies (page 125)

CHOCOLATE-CHERRY SAND TARTS

¾ cup sugar

¾ cup margarine or butter, softened

1 egg white

1¾ cups all-purpose flour

¼ cup cocoa

About 1¾ cups cherry preserves

Chocolate Glaze (below)

Mix sugar, margarine and egg white in large bowl. Stir in flour and cocoa. Cover and refrigerate about 2 hours or until firm.

Heat oven to 350°. Press 1-inch ball of dough in bottom and up side of each ungreased sandbakelse mold, about 1¾ × ½ inch. Spoon about 1½ teaspoons cherry preserves into each mold. Place on cookie sheet. Bake 12 to 15 minutes or until crust is set. Cool about 10 minutes. Carefully remove cookies from molds. Cool completely. Prepare Chocolate Glaze and drizzle on cookies. **About 4½ dozen cookies.**

CHOCOLATE GLAZE

⅔ cup semisweet chocolate chips

1 tablespoon shortening

Heat and stir ingredients until melted and smooth.

LACY COOKIE CUPS

½ cup powdered sugar

¼ cup butter*

½ teaspoon vanilla

2 egg whites

¼ cup all-purpose flour

¼ teaspoon ground cinnamon

2 cups mixed fresh strawberries and raspberries

⅓ cup raspberry jam, melted

Heat oven to 400°. Generously grease cookie sheet. Beat powdered sugar, butter and vanilla in medium bowl until well blended. Beat in egg whites until mixture is well blended but not foamy. Fold in flour and cinnamon.

Spoon about 1½ tablespoons dough at a time 6 inches apart on cookie sheet. Flatten into 5-inch rounds using back of spoon dipped in cold water. Bake 5 to 6 minutes or until golden brown. Let stand 30 seconds or until firm. Immediately remove from cookie sheet. Shape cookie over inverted 6-ounce custard cup. Cool completely. Fill each cookie cup with about ⅓ cup berries. Drizzle with raspberry jam. **About 6 cookie cups.**

Margarine is not recommended for this recipe.

ROSETTES

Be sure the rosette iron is hot enough or the batter will stick. Test the first rosette for crispness. If it isn't crisp enough, the batter is too thick; stir in a small amount of water or milk, about one or two tablespoons.

1 tablespoon sugar	½ cup water or milk
½ teaspoon salt	1 tablespoon vegetable oil
1 egg	Vegetable oil
½ cup all-purpose flour	Glaze (below) or powdered sugar

Beat sugar, salt and egg in deep 1½ quart bowl on medium speed. Beat in flour, water and 1 tablespoon oil until smooth. Heat oil (2 to 3 inches) in 3-quart saucepan to 400°.

Heat rosette iron before making each cookie by placing in hot oil 1 minute. Tap excess oil from iron onto paper towel. Dip hot iron into batter just to top edge (don't go over top). Fry about 30 seconds or until golden brown. Immediately remove rosette. Invert onto paper towel to cool. Just before serving, prepare Glaze. Dip rosettes into Glaze or sprinkle with powdered sugar. **About 2 dozen rosettes.**

GLAZE

1½ cups powdered sugar	½ teaspoon grated orange or lemon peel or
3 tablespoons milk	½ teaspoon vanilla or
	¼ teaspoon almond extract
	Food color, if desired

Mix all ingredients in deep 1½-quart bowl until smooth.

SNOWFLAKES

Cut these snowflake cookies just as you would fold paper snowflakes. Canapé cutters can also be used to cut designs in the dough.

3 eggs, beaten

2 tablespoons vegetable oil

½ teaspoon baking powder

¼ teaspoon salt

1¾ to 2 cups all-purpose flour

Vegetable oil

Powdered sugar

Mix eggs, 2 tablespoons oil, the baking powder and salt in large bowl. Gradually stir in enough flour to make a very stiff dough. Knead 5 minutes.

Heat oil (at least 1 inch deep) in Dutch oven to 375°. Roll half of dough at a time as thin as possible on well-floured surface, turning dough frequently to prevent sticking. (Dough will bounce back. Continue rolling until it stays stretched out.)

With pastry wheel, knife or cookie cutter, cut dough into 3-inch squares, hexagons or circles. Fold pieces into fourths. Cut random designs into edges (as for paper snowflakes).* Fry opened dough pieces, two or three at a time, about 30 seconds or until delicate brown. Turn quickly and brown other side. Drain on paper towels. Sprinkle with powdered sugar just before serving. **About 3½ dozen cookies.**

Cut all pieces before starting to fry and place on lightly floured surface.

Rosettes (page 129), Snowflakes

Specialty Cookies

CHAPTER SEVEN
HOLIDAY AND PARTY COOKIES

▼■▼■▼■▼■▼■▼■▼■▼■▼■▼■▼■▼■▼■▼■▼■▼■

No one needs an excuse to bake cookies; still, there are times when the baking of cookies is little short of ritual, and holidays head that list. Many different cookies celebrate the holidays, and included are some of our favorites in honor of Christmas, Halloween, Thanksgiving, Valentine's Day and Purim.

The most whimsical, the most elegant and the most casual party cookies are all also here just for the most delicious parties.

▼■▼■▼■▼■▼■▼■▼■▼■▼■▼■▼■▼■▼■▼■▼■▼■

THE ULTIMATE
VALENTINE'S DAY COOKIE

1 cup powdered sugar

1 cup margarine or butter, softened

1 tablespoon vinegar

2¼ cups all-purpose flour

1½ teaspoons ground ginger

¾ teaspoon baking soda

¼ teaspoon salt

6 drops red food color

Heat oven to 400°. Mix powdered sugar, margarine and vinegar in large bowl. Stir in remaining ingredients except food color. Divide dough in half. Mix food color into one half. (If dough is too dry, work in milk, 1 teaspoon at a time.) Roll dough ⅛ inch thick on lightly floured cloth-covered surface. Cut into various size heart shapes with cookie cutters. Mix and match sizes and colors. Place about 2 inches apart on ungreased cookie sheet. Bake 5 to 7 minutes or until set but not brown. Cool slightly. Carefully remove from cookie sheet. Cool completely. Decorate with white and pink Decorator's Frosting (page 5) if desired.

▼■▼■▼■▼■▼■▼■▼■▼■▼■▼■▼■▼■▼■▼■▼■▼■

The Ultimate Valentine's Day Cookie, Chocolate Linzer Hearts (page 134)

CHOCOLATE LINZER HEARTS

1 cup margarine or butter

½ cup sugar

2 eggs

1 teaspoon vanilla

2½ cups all-purpose flour

1 cup hazelnuts, toasted, skinned and ground

1½ teaspoons ground cinnamon

½ teaspoon ground nutmeg

½ ounce semisweet chocolate, finely chopped

½ cup raspberry jam

1 ounce semisweet chocolate, melted

Beat margarine and sugar in large bowl until light and fluffy. Beat in eggs and vanilla until smooth. Add remaining ingredients except jam and melted chocolate. Beat until well blended. Cover and refrigerate dough 1 hour. (Dough will be sticky.)

Heat oven to 375°. Roll one-fourth of dough at a time ⅛ inch thick on lightly floured surface. (Keep remaining dough refrigerated until ready to roll.)

Cut with 2-inch heart-shaped cookie cutter. Cut out centers of half the cookies, if desired. Place on ungreased cookie sheet. Bake 7 to 9 minutes or until light brown. Remove from cookie sheet. Cool completely. Put cookies together in pairs with about ½ teaspoon raspberry jam each. Drizzle with melted chocolate. **3 dozen sandwich cookies.**

LEBKUCHEN

These Christmas honey cakes were first popular in the Black Forest region of Germany.

½ cup honey

½ cup molasses

¾ cup packed brown sugar

1 egg

1 teaspoon grated lemon peel

1 tablespoon lemon juice

2¾ cups all-purpose flour

⅓ cup cut-up citron

⅓ cup chopped nuts

1 teaspoon ground cinnamon

1 teaspoon ground cloves

1 teaspoon ground allspice

1 teaspoon ground nutmeg

½ teaspoon baking soda

Glazing Icing (below)

Heat honey and molasses to boiling in 1-quart saucepan. Remove from heat; cool completely. Mix honey-molasses mixture, brown sugar, egg, lemon peel and lemon juice in large bowl. Stir in remaining ingredients except Glazing Icing. Cover and refrigerate for 8 hours or overnight.

Prepare Glazing Icing. Heat oven to 400°. Grease cookie sheet. Roll one-fourth of dough at a time ¼ inch thick on lightly floured cloth-covered surface. Cut into rectangles, 2½ × 1½ inches. Place 1 inch apart on cookie sheet. Bake 10 to 12 minutes or until no indentation remains when touched in center. Brush icing lightly over cookies. Immediately remove from baking sheet. Cool completely. **About 5 dozen cookies.**

GLAZING ICING

1 cup granulated sugar

½ cup water

¼ cup powdered sugar

Mix granulated sugar and water in 1-quart saucepan. Cook over medium heat to 230° or just until small amount of mixture spins 2-inch thread. Remove from heat. Stir in powdered sugar. If icing becomes sugary while brushing cookies, reheat slightly, adding a little water until clear again. Any leftover icing may be used on fruitcake or other fruit bars.

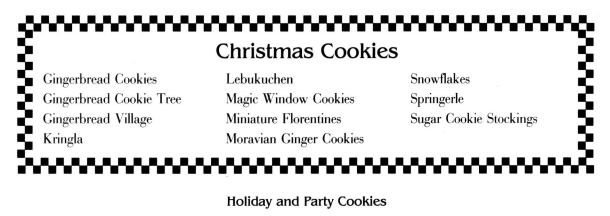

Christmas Cookies

Gingerbread Cookies	Lebukuchen	Snowflakes
Gingerbread Cookie Tree	Magic Window Cookies	Springerle
Gingerbread Village	Miniature Florentines	Sugar Cookie Stockings
Kringla	Moravian Ginger Cookies	

Sugar Cookie Stockings

The Ultimate Sugar Cookie (page 51)

Food colors, if desired

Thin Cookie Glaze (below) or Decorator's Frosting (page 5)

Prepare and refrigerate dough as directed, adding desired food colors.

Heat oven to 375°. Roll one-third of dough at a time 3⁄16 inch thick on lightly floured cloth-covered surface. Cut into 6- to 8-inch stockings. (To enlarge pattern, see directions below.) If desired, cut toy-shaped cookies to stick out of tops of stockings.

Place stockings on ungreased cookie sheet. Cut accent dough (toes, heels, cuffs) to place on stockings if desired. Bake about 9 minutes or until light brown. Cool 1 to 2 minutes. Remove from cookie sheet. Cool completely. Glaze and decorate cookies with Thin Cookie Glaze or decorate with Decorator's Frosting. **7 to 12 stockings.**

Thin Cookie Glaze

2 cups powdered sugar

2 tablespoons milk

1⁄4 teaspoon almond extract

Red or green food color

About 1⁄3 cup powdered sugar

Mix 2 cups powdered sugar, the milk, and almond extract. Tint half of the mixture with 4 or 5 drops food color. Add additional milk, a few drops at a time, if necessary for glaze consistency. Place baked cookies on wire rack. Pour small amount of glaze over each cookie; spread to edge with spatula. Add enough powdered sugar to remaining glaze to make frosting that can be used in a decorating bag and will hold its shape. Place in decorating bag with **#2** writing tip. Decorate cookies as desired. **Enough to glaze and decorate 8 to 10 stockings.**

To Enlarge Pattern: Make a grid of the desired size and draw in the pattern, square by square, exactly as it appears below. Cut out the enlarged design and use it as your pattern.

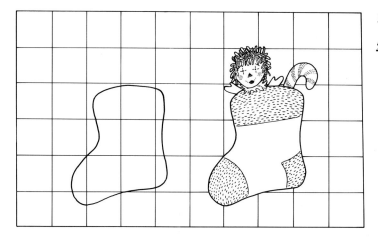

1. *Enlarge grid to desired size and draw in stocking pattern.*
2. *Add toy-shaped cookies to top of stocking and accent dough to toes, heels and cuffs if desired.*

Sugar Cookie Stockings

MINIATURE FLORENTINES

Watch these little cookies carefully because they darken quickly.

½ cup sugar

¼ cup margarine or butter

¼ cup whipping (heavy) cream

2 tablespoons honey

½ cup sliced almonds

¼ cup candied orange peel, finely chopped

1 tablespoon grated orange peel

1 package (4 ounces) sweet cooking chocolate, melted

Heat oven to 375°. Line cookie sheet with cooking parchment paper. Mix sugar, margarine, whipping cream and honey in 2½-quart saucepan. Heat mixture to boiling, stirring constantly. Boil and stir 5 minutes; remove from heat. Stir in remaining ingredients except chocolate. Let stand 5 minutes.

Drop mixture by ½ teaspoonfuls 2 inches apart onto cookie sheet. Bake 4 to 6 minutes or until golden brown and bubbly. Cool 2 minutes or until firm. Remove from cookie sheet. Cool completely.

Turn cookies upside down; brush with melted chocolate. Let stand at room temperature until chocolate is set. **About 6 dozen cookies.**

GINGERBREAD VILLAGE

Decorate the buildings—a bank, grocery, hardware store, dress shop, library—any way you like. Use red cinnamon candies, licorice bits and whips, jelly candies, jelly beans, pillow mints, peppermints and whatever else strikes your fancy. Sliced almonds are wonderful masonry or paving stones. Make an old-fashioned lamppost from a peppermint stick, with small gingerbread squares as the lantern top.

½ cup packed brown sugar

¼ cup shortening

¾ cup dark molasses

⅓ cup cold water

3½ cups all-purpose flour

1 teaspoon baking soda

1 teaspoon ground ginger

½ teaspoon salt

½ teaspoon ground allspice

½ teaspoon ground cloves

½ teaspoon ground cinnamon

Frosting (page 139)

Assorted candies and nuts

Cardboard, 28 × 10 inches

Heat oven to 350°. Grease square pan, 9 × 9 × 2 inches, and jelly roll pan, 15½ × 10½ × 1 inch. Mix brown sugar, shortening and molasses in large bowl. Stir in water. (Mixture will look curdled.) Stir in flour, baking soda, ginger, salt, allspice, cloves and cinnamon.

Press one-third of dough into square pan with slightly floured fingers. Press remaining dough into jelly roll pan. Bake, 1 pan at a time, about 15 minutes or until no indentation remains when touched in center. Cool 5 minutes. Invert onto large cutting surface. Immediately cut jelly roll into fourths and then into buildings as shown below. Cut square into braces as shown. Cool completely.

Cover cardboard with aluminum foil. Prepare Frosting. Decorate front of buildings as desired using frosting and assorted candies and nuts. Use frosting to attach supports to backs of buildings, buildings to cardboard and sidewalk to cardboard. Complete by decorating as desired. **1 (four-building) village.**

FROSTING

2 cups powdered sugar

⅓ cup shortening

2 tablespoons light corn syrup

5 to 6 teaspoons milk

Mix all ingredients until smooth and of desired consistency.

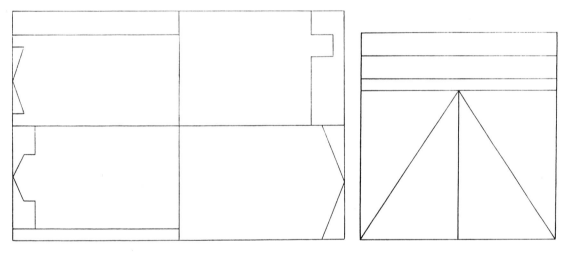

Cut jelly roll into fourths and then into buildings.

Cut square into braces.

HAMANTASCHEN

These rich, filled cookies celebrate the holiday of Purim, which honors the victory of the Jews of ancient Persia over Haman's plot to destroy them. Haman was an adviser to King Ahasuerus, and Hamantaschen are "Haman's pockets." Some Hamantaschen recipes call for a yeast-raised or sour cream dough; we use a short crust dough for tender results.

2½ cups all-purpose flour

½ cup sugar

1 teaspoon baking powder

¾ cup margarine or butter

1 teaspoon grated lemon peel

½ teaspoon vanilla

2 eggs

Prune, Apricot, Plum or Poppy Seed Filling (below)

Mix flour, sugar and baking powder in large bowl. Cut in margarine until mixture resembles fine crumbs. Mix lemon peel, vanilla and eggs. Stir into flour mixture until dough forms a ball. (Use hands to combine all ingredients if necessary. Add up to ¼ cup additional flour if dough is too sticky to handle.) Cover and refrigerate 2 hours or until firm. Heat oven to 350°. Roll half of dough at a time ⅛ inch thick on lightly floured cloth-covered surface. Cut into 3-inch rounds. Spoon 1 level teaspoon filling onto each round. Bring up 3 sides with metal spatula to form triangle around filling. Pinch edges together firmly. Place about 2 inches apart on ungreased cookie sheet. Bake 12 to 15 minutes or until light brown. Immediately remove from cookie sheet. **About 4 dozen cookies.**

PRUNE FILLING

1 package (12 ounces) pitted prunes

1 cup chopped walnuts

2 tablespoons honey

1 tablespoon lemon juice

Bring prunes and enough water to cover to boil in 2-quart saucepan; reduce heat. Cover and simmer 10 minutes. Drain well and mash. Stir in remaining ingredients.

APRICOT OR PLUM FILLING

1½ cups apricot or plum jam

½ cup finely chopped almonds or walnuts

1 teaspoon grated lemon peel

1 tablespoon lemon juice

About ½ cup dry bread crumbs

Mix jam, almonds, lemon peel and lemon juice. Stir in just enough bread crumbs until thickened.

POPPY SEED FILLING

1 cup poppy seed

¼ cup walnut pieces

1 tablespoon margarine or butter

1 tablespoon honey

1 teaspoon lemon juice

1 egg white

Place all ingredients in blender or food processor. Cover and blend or process until smooth.

Hamantaschen, Esther's Bracelets (page 144)

ESTHER'S BRACELETS

It was Queen Esther who revealed the evil plot of Haman to King Ahasuerus of ancient Persia, thereby saving the Persian Jews. These almond cookies honor her.

1 cup sugar	2 eggs
¾ cup margarine or butter, softened	4 cups all-purpose flour
¾ cup shortening	½ cup finely chopped almonds
½ teaspoon almond extract	Glaze (below)

Heat oven to 375°. Mix sugar, margarine, shortening, almond extract and eggs in large bowl. Stir in flour and almonds.

Shape dough into 1¼-inch balls. Roll each ball into rope, 6 inches long. Form each rope into circle, crossing ends and tucking under. Place on ungreased cookie sheet. Bake 9 to 11 minutes or until set but not brown. Remove from cookie sheet. Cool completely. Prepare Glaze and drizzle on cookies. Sprinkle with additional finely chopped almonds if desired. **About 6 dozen cookies.**

GLAZE

3 cups powdered sugar

4 to 5 tablespoons milk

Mix all ingredients until of drizzling consistency.

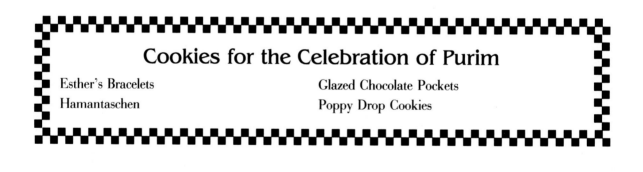

Cookies for the Celebration of Purim

Esther's Bracelets	Glazed Chocolate Pockets
Hamantaschen	Poppy Drop Cookies

FROSTED PUMPKIN-PECAN COOKIES

Soft and cinnamon-kissed, these pumpkin cookies celebrate the plenty of harvest time.

1½ cups packed brown sugar

½ cup margarine or butter, softened

½ cup shortening

1 cup canned pumpkin

1 egg

2⅓ cups all-purpose flour

1 teaspoon baking powder

½ teaspoon salt

½ teaspoon ground cinnamon

2 cups chopped pecans

Frosting (below)

Heat oven to 350°. Mix brown sugar, margarine and shortening in large bowl. Stir in pumpkin and egg. Stir in flour, baking powder, salt and cinnamon. Stir in pecans.

Drop by rounded tablespoonfuls about 2 inches apart onto ungreased cookie sheet; flatten slightly. Bake 12 to 15 minutes or until no indentation remains when touched lightly in center. Remove from cookie sheet. Cool completely. Prepare Frosting and spread each cookie with about 1 teaspoon. **About 5 dozen cookies.**

FROSTING

3 cups powdered sugar

¼ cup margarine or butter, softened

3 to 4 tablespoons milk

¼ teaspoon ground cinnamon

Mix all ingredients until smooth and of desired consistency.

CRANBERRY-ORANGE COOKIES

Cranberries are harvested in the autumn, but can be found year 'round in supermarkets. With all the lovely flavors of a holiday cranberry quickbread, these cookies are soft-centered with slightly crunchy edges.

1 cup granulated sugar	2½ cups all-purpose flour
½ cup packed brown sugar	2 cups coarsely chopped cranberries
1 cup margarine or butter, softened	½ cup chopped nuts, if desired
1 teaspoon grated orange peel	½ teaspoon baking soda
2 tablespoons orange juice	½ teaspoon salt
1 egg	Orange Glaze (below)

Heat oven to 375°. Mix sugars, margarine, orange peel, orange juice and egg in large bowl. Stir in remaining ingredients except Orange Glaze.

Drop by rounded tablespoonfuls about 2 inches apart onto ungreased cookie sheet. Bake 12 to 14 minutes or until light brown. Remove from cookie sheet. Cool completely. Prepare Orange Glaze and spread each cookie with about ½ teaspoon. **About 4 dozen cookies.**

ORANGE GLAZE

1½ cups powdered sugar

3 tablespoons orange juice

½ teaspoon grated orange peel

Mix all ingredients until smooth.

Halloween Cookies

CANDY CORN SHORTBREAD

These are very cute, just like the Halloween candy children love so much.

¾ cup margarine or butter, softened

¼ cup sugar

2 cups all-purpose flour

Yellow food color

Red food color

Mix margarine and sugar in large bowl. Stir in flour. Divide dough into six equal parts. Combine 3 parts dough and mix with 10 drops yellow and 4 drops red food color (for orange). Mix 2 parts dough with 7 drops yellow food color (for yellow).

Pat orange dough into ¾ inch-thick rectangle, 9 × 2 inches, on plastic wrap. Pat yellow dough into ½ inch-thick rectangle, 9 × 1¾ inches. Place lengthwise in center on top of orange rectangle. Roll remaining part dough into roll, 9 × ¾ inch. Place lengthwise in center on top of yellow rectangle. Wrap plastic wrap around dough, pressing dough into triangle. Refrigerate 2 hours or until firm.

Heat oven to 350°. Cut wedge of dough into ¼-inch slices. Place about 1 inch apart on ungreased cookie sheet. Bake 10 to 12 minutes or until set. Remove from cookie sheet.
About 3 dozen cookies.

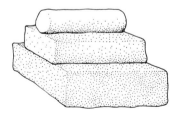

Stack dough so that the orange rectangle is on the bottom and the uncolored roll of dough is on top.

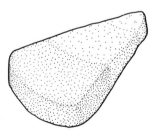

Press dough into triangle so that sliced wedges resemble a kernel of corn.

MAGIC WINDOW COOKIES

Use Halloween cookie cutters and cut out sections to be filled with hard candy. When making the "magic windows," try different colors of candy. Place candy pieces to form stripes, polka dots and swirls.

1 cup sugar

¾ cup margarine or butter

2 eggs

1 teaspoon vanilla or ½ teaspoon lemon extract

2½ cups all-purpose flour

1 teaspoon baking powder

¼ teaspoon salt

5 ounces fruit-flavored hard candy, chopped

Mix sugar, margarine, eggs and vanilla in large bowl. Stir in flour, baking powder and salt. Cover and refrigerate 1 hour or until firm.

Heat oven to 375°. Line cookie sheet with aluminum foil. Roll one-third of dough at a time ⅛ inch thick on lightly floured surface. Cut into desired Halloween shapes with cookie cutters. Cut out designs from cookies using smaller cutters or your own patterns. Place pieces of candy in cutouts, mixing colors as desired.

Bake cookies 7 to 9 minutes or until very light brown and candy is melted. If candy has not filled out cutout design, immediately spread hot candy with knife. Cool completely on cookie sheet. Gently remove cookies. **About 6 dozen 3-inch cookies.**

Cookies for a Springtime Tea

Almond Bonbons

Chocolate Chip Shortbread Cookies

Cream Wafers

Hazelnut Sablés

Lemon-Lime Cookies

Lemon Tea Biscuits

Oatmeal Lacies

Orange-Almond Pillows

Orange Madeleines

Raspberry Logs

Sunflower Cookies

Magic Window Cookies, Candy Corn Shortbread (page 147)

Hazelnut Sablés

Pronounced "sah-blay," sablés are French cookies that translate to "sandies." They are rich, short cookies with pronounced hazelnut flavor.

¾ **cup margarine or butter, softened**	½ **cup hazelnuts, toasted and ground**
¾ **cup powdered sugar**	1 **egg, beaten**
½ **teaspoon vanilla**	¼ **cup chopped hazelnuts**
1 **egg yolk**	¼ **cup sanding sugar**
1¼ **cups all-purpose flour**	

Beat margarine and powdered sugar in large bowl until light and fluffy. Stir in vanilla and egg yolk. Stir in flour and ground hazelnuts until well blended. Cover tightly and refrigerate 1 hour.

Heat oven to 350°. Roll one-fourth of dough at a time ¼ inch thick on lightly floured surface. (Keep remaining dough refrigerated until ready to roll.) Cut into 2½-inch rounds. Place about 2 inches apart on ungreased cookie sheet. Brush with egg. Sprinkle with chopped hazelnuts and sugar. Bake 8 to 10 minutes or until edges are light brown. Remove from cookie sheet. **About 3 dozen cookies.**

Lemon Tea Biscuits

Assemble these light wafers with the tart lemon filling no longer than an hour or two before serving—they soften on standing. Because they are quite English, we call them by the British name for cookie: "biscuit." Unfilled cookies can be frozen (see page 4) until needed. For a card party, cut the dough into hearts, diamonds, clubs and spades.

1 **cup margarine or butter**	2 **cups all-purpose flour**
½ **cup sugar**	½ **cup ground pecans**
1 **tablespoon grated lemon peel**	1 **cup lemon curd or pie filling**
¼ **teaspoon salt**	**Lemon Glaze (page 151)**
1 **egg**	

Mix margarine, sugar, lemon peel, salt and egg in large bowl until well blended. Stir in flour and pecans. Cover and refrigerate 1 hour or until firm.

Heat oven to 350°. Roll half of dough at a time about ⅛ inch thick on floured surface. Cut into 2-inch rounds. Place on ungreased cookie sheet. Bake 7 to 9 minutes or until edges are just barely brown. Remove from cookie sheet. Cool completely. Put cookies together in pairs using rounded teaspoonful lemon curd for filling. Prepare Lemon Glaze and brush on tops of cookies. **4 dozen sandwich cookies.**

LEMON GLAZE

¼ cup powdered sugar

1 teaspoon grated lemon peel

2 teaspoons lemon juice

Mix all ingredients.

ORANGE-ALMOND PILLOWS

These little puffs really look like pillows. For crisp cookies, bake until light brown. For chewy cookies, bake just until set—not brown.

1½ cups blanched almonds, ground

1 tablespoon grated orange peel

1 egg white

½ cup powdered sugar

Orange Glaze (below)

Heat oven to 350°. Grease and flour cookie sheet or line with cooking parchment paper. Mix almonds and orange peel; reserve. Beat egg white in medium bowl on high speed until stiff but not dry. Gradually beat in powdered sugar. Beat on high speed about 3 minutes or until slightly stiff. Fold almond mixture into egg white mixture (mixture will be stiff).

Roll dough into rectangle, 9 × 6 inches, on cloth-covered surface generously dusted with powdered sugar. Cut into 1½-inch squares. Place 1 inch apart on cookie sheet. Bake 10 to 12 minutes or until set and very light brown. Remove from cookie sheet. Cool completely. Prepare Orange Glaze and drizzle on cookies. **2 dozen cookies.**

ORANGE GLAZE

¾ cup powdered sugar

3 to 4 teaspoons orange juice

¼ teaspoon grated orange peel

Mix ingredients until smooth and of desired consistency.

Left: Hazelnut Sables (page 150), Orange-Almond Pillows (page 151), Right: Lemon Tea Biscuits (pages 150–151)

SPICY SEASCAPE COOKIES

¾ cup margarine or butter

⅔ cup powdered sugar

2 tablespoons light molasses

1 egg

2 cups all-purpose flour

2 teaspoons ground cardamom

1½ teaspoons ground cinnamon

1 teaspoon baking soda

Thin Glaze (below)

Cocoa

Heat oven to 325°. Grease cookie sheet. Mix margarine, powdered sugar, molasses and egg in large bowl. Stir in flour, cardamom, cinnamon and baking soda. Roll one-third of dough ⅛ inch thick on lightly floured board. Shape into sand dollars, starfish and scallops as directed below. Bake 7 to 9 minutes or until light brown. Remove from cookie sheet. Cool completely. Prepare Thin Glaze and decorate cookies as directed. **About 4½ dozen cookies.**

Sand dollars: Cut dough with round 3-inch cutter. Place on cookie sheet. Draw five-pointed star in middle of circle. Make small hole in center and indentations at edge of circle. After baking, brush with Thin Glaze (white); sprinkle with granulated sugar if desired.

Starfish: Cut dough with five-pointed star-shaped cutter. Place on cookie sheet. Curve points of stars and make indentations down center of each starfish "arm" with knife. After baking, brush with colored glaze.

Scallops: Cut dough with scalloped 2½-inch round cutter. Cut 2 small wedges off bottom of circle forming base of shell. Using knife, draw curved lines across top to form shell pattern. After baking, brush with colored glaze. While glaze is still wet, lightly sprinkle with cocoa; brush to make marbled effect.

THIN GLAZE

¾ cup powdered sugar

1 tablespoon plus 1½ teaspoons hot water

Peach or coral paste food color

Mix all ingredients until of uniform color. If glaze becomes too stiff, add additional hot water, ½ teaspoon at a time.

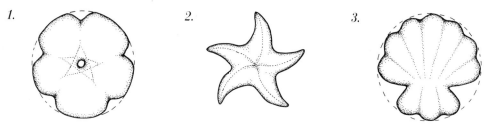

1. Draw five-pointed star in middle of circle, make small hole in center and indent edges to form sand dollar.
2. Curve tips of star and make indentations down center of each arm to form starfish.
3. Cut 2 small wedges off bottom of circle and draw curved lines across top to form shell pattern on scallop.

ORANGE SLICES

"Sanding" sugar is coarse decorating sugar found in specialty shops.

1½ cups powdered sugar

1 cup margarine or butter, softened

1 egg

1 tablespoon grated orange peel

1 teaspoon vanilla

2¾ cups all-purpose flour

1 teaspoon baking soda

1 teaspoon cream of tartar

Orange sanding sugar

Frosting (below)

Mix powdered sugar and margarine in large bowl. Stir in egg, orange peel and vanilla. Stir in remaining ingredients except sanding sugar and Frosting. Cover and refrigerate 1 hour or until firm.

Heat oven to 375°. Roll half of dough at a time ⅛ inch thick on lightly floured surface. Cut into 3-inch rounds; cut rounds in half. Place on ungreased cookie sheet. Sprinkle with sanding sugar. Bake 7 to 8 minutes or until light brown. Remove from cookie sheet. Cool completely.

Prepare Frosting and place in decorating bag with #3 writing tip. Outline orange segments on cookies. **About 6 dozen cookies.**

FROSTING

2 cups powdered sugar

About 2 tablespoons half-and-half

½ teaspoon vanilla

Beat ingredients until smooth.

GOLDFISH DROPS

The enticing combination of salty and sweet is one that "big kids" will go for too.

1 cup butterscotch chips

1 tablespoon shortening

1 package (6 ounces) goldfish crackers (about 3½ cups)

1 cup broken pretzel sticks

Butter cookie sheets. Heat butterscotch chips and shortening in 3-quart saucepan over low heat, stirring constantly, until butterscotch chips are melted and mixture is smooth. Remove from heat. Stir in crackers and pretzels until well coated.

Drop mixture by rounded tablespoonfuls onto cookie sheet. Let stand 1 hour or until firm. Carefully remove from cookie sheet. **About 3 dozen cookies.**

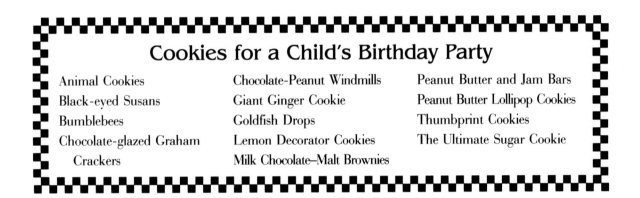

Cookies for a Child's Birthday Party

Animal Cookies

Black-eyed Susans

Bumblebees

Chocolate-glazed Graham
    Crackers

Chocolate-Peanut Windmills

Giant Ginger Cookie

Goldfish Drops

Lemon Decorator Cookies

Milk Chocolate–Malt Brownies

Peanut Butter and Jam Bars

Peanut Butter Lollipop Cookies

Thumbprint Cookies

The Ultimate Sugar Cookie

PEANUT BUTTER LOLLIPOP COOKIES

Children find these cookies enchanting. Decorate them any way you like, with faces, names or abstract designs.

½ cup granulated sugar

½ cup packed brown sugar

½ cup creamy peanut butter

½ cup margarine or butter, softened

¼ cup shortening

1 egg

1⅔ cups all-purpose flour

¾ teaspoon baking soda

½ teaspoon baking powder

¼ teaspoon salt

25 to 30 wooden ice cream or lollipop sticks

Glaze (below)

Chocolate sprinkles

Decorator Frosting (below)

Mix sugars, peanut butter, margarine, shortening and egg in large bowl. Stir in flour, baking soda, baking powder and salt. Cover and refrigerate about 1 hour or until firm.

Heat oven to 375°. Roll half of dough at a time ⅛ inch thick on floured cloth-covered surface with cloth-covered rolling pin. Cut into 2½-inch rounds. Place about 3 inches apart on ungreased cookie sheet. Lightly press sticks onto rounds to form 2½-inch handles. Top each with another round; gently press to seal. Bake 10 to 11 minutes or until light brown. Cool slightly; remove from cookie sheet. Cool completely.

Prepare Glaze and spread evenly on top of one cookie at a time. Immediately coat edge with chocolate sprinkles. Repeat with remaining cookies. Prepare Decorator Frosting and place in decorating bag with #3 or #4 writing tip and decorate cookies. **2 to 2½ dozen cookies.**

GLAZE

2 cups powdered sugar

2 tablespoons water

2 tablespoons light corn syrup

Mix all ingredients in saucepan until smooth. Heat over low heat just until lukewarm (1 to 2 minutes); remove from heat. If necessary, add hot water, a few drops at a time, until of spreading consistency.

DECORATOR FROSTING

1 cup powdered sugar

1 tablespoon creamy peanut butter

3 to 4 teaspoons milk

½ teaspoon cocoa

Mix all ingredients until smooth and of piping consistency.

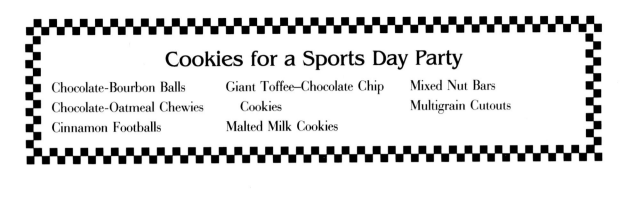

CINNAMON FOOTBALLS

½ cup packed brown sugar

½ cup margarine or butter, softened

1 teaspoon vanilla

1½ cups all-purpose flour

½ teaspoon ground cinnamon

⅛ teaspoon salt

About 24 whole blanched almonds

Decorating Glaze (below)

Heat oven to 350°. Mix brown sugar, margarine and vanilla in large bowl. Work in flour, cinnamon and salt until dough holds together. (If dough is dry, mix in 1 to 2 tablespoons milk.)

Shape dough by scant tablespoonfuls around almonds to form football shapes. Place about 1 inch apart on ungreased cookie sheet. Bake 12 to 14 minutes or until set but not brown. Remove from cookie sheet. Cool completely. Prepare Decorating Glaze and place in decorating bag with #3 writing tip. Make football laces on cookies. **About 2 dozen cookies.**

DECORATING GLAZE

½ cup powdered sugar

1½ to 3 teaspoons water

Mix powdered sugar and just enough water to make paste that can be piped from decorating bag.

Cinnamon Baseballs: Substitute pitted dates, cut in half crosswise, for the almonds. Mold dough around date half into baseball shape. Pipe on laces.

MULTIGRAIN CUTOUTS

Perfect for a sports party, these hearty cookies have a nutty, not-too-sweet flavor. The "dump" method of mixing all the ingredients together makes these cookies supereasy.

3¼ cups whole wheat flour

1 cup sugar

⅔ cup shortening

¼ cup cornmeal

¼ cup wheat germ

¾ cup milk

1 teaspoon baking powder

½ teaspoon salt

½ teaspoon vanilla

Baked-on Frosting (below)

Heat oven to 350°. Mix all ingredients except Baked-on Frosting.

Roll about one-third of dough at a time ⅛ inch thick on lightly floured surface. Cut with sport-shaped cookie cutters. Place on ungreased cookie sheet. Prepare Baked-on Frosting and place in decorating bag with #5 writing tip. Outline or decorate unbaked cookies. Bake 12 to 14 minutes or until edges are light brown. Cool slightly. Remove from cookie sheet.

About 6 dozen 2- to 3-inch cookies.

BAKED-ON FROSTING

⅔ cup all-purpose flour

⅔ cup margarine or butter, softened

1 tablespoon hot water

Mix flour and margarine until smooth. Stir in hot water.

Cinnamon Footballs (page 159), Multigrain Cutouts

CHAPTER EIGHT

THE ALL-OCCASION BROWNIE

■▼■▼■▼■▼■▼■▼■▼■▼■▼■▼■▼■▼■▼■▼■▼■

It isn't easy to imagine life before brownies, but there was a time—before the 1920s—when they weren't the roaringly popular bar cookie we know and love today. Brownies are in a class by themselves. They may be fudgy or cakelike, with nuts or without, and even though they are most frequently thought of as being chocolate, we also give you brownies in a rich array of flavors from raspberry and amaretto all the way to vanilla.

■▼■▼■▼■▼■▼■▼■▼■▼■▼■▼■▼■▼■▼■▼■▼■

THE ULTIMATE
BROWNIE

5 squares (1 ounce each) unsweetened chocolate

⅔ cup margarine or butter

1¾ cups sugar

2 teaspoons vanilla

3 eggs

1 cup all-purpose flour

1 cup chopped nuts

1 cup (6 ounces) semisweet chocolate chips, if desired

Heat oven to 350°. Grease square pan, 9 × 9 × 2 inches. Heat chocolate and margarine over low heat, stirring frequently, until melted; remove from heat. Cool slightly. Beat sugar, vanilla and eggs in large bowl on high speed 5 minutes. Beat in chocolate mixture on low speed. Beat in flour just until blended. Stir in nuts and chocolate chips.

Spread batter in pan. Bake 40 to 45 minutes or just until brownies begin to pull away from sides of pan. Cool completely. Spread with Chocolate Frosting (page 27) if desired. **24 brownies.**

■▼■▼■▼■▼■▼■▼■▼■▼■▼■▼■▼■▼■▼■▼■▼■

The Ultimate Brownie, Milk Chocolate–Malt Brownies (page 166)

FUDGY SAUCEPAN BROWNIES

1 package (12 ounces) semisweet chocolate chips

½ cup margarine or butter

1⅔ cups sugar

1¼ cups all-purpose flour

1 teaspoon vanilla

½ teaspoon baking powder

½ teaspoon salt

3 eggs

1 cup chopped nuts, if desired

Heat oven to 350°. Heat chocolate chips and margarine in 3-quart saucepan over low heat, stirring constantly, until melted; remove from heat. Stir in remaining ingredients except nuts. Stir in nuts.

Spread batter in ungreased rectangular pan, 13 × 9 × 2 inches. Bake 25 to 30 minutes or until center is set. Cool completely. **32 brownies.**

COCOA BROWNIES

This is the one for all those people who like cakelike, tender brownies.

1 cup sugar

½ cup shortening

1 teaspoon vanilla

2 eggs

⅔ cup all-purpose flour

½ cup cocoa

½ teaspoon baking powder

¼ teaspoon salt

½ cup chopped walnuts, if desired

Heat oven to 350°. Grease square pan, 9 × 9 × 2 inches. Mix sugar, shortening, vanilla and eggs in large bowl. Stir in remaining ingredients except nuts. Stir in nuts.

Spread batter in pan. Bake 20 to 25 minutes or until toothpick inserted in center comes out clean. Cool completely. **16 brownies.**

Turtle Brownies: Omit walnuts. Sprinkle ½ cup coarsely chopped pecans over batter before baking. Bake as directed. Heat 12 vanilla caramels and 1 tablespoon milk over low heat, stirring frequently, until caramels are melted. Drizzle over warm brownies. Cool completely.

Turtle Brownies

MILK CHOCOLATE—MALT BROWNIES

This luscious brownie is almost a candy confection.

1 package (11.5 ounces) milk chocolate chips

½ cup margarine or butter

¾ cup sugar

1 teaspoon vanilla

3 eggs

1¾ cups all-purpose flour

½ cup instant malted milk

½ teaspoon baking powder

¼ teaspoon salt

1 cup malted milk balls, coarsely chopped

Heat oven to 350°. Grease rectangular pan, 13 × 9 × 2 inches. Heat milk chocolate and margarine in 3-quart saucepan over low heat, stirring frequently, until melted; remove from heat. Cool slightly. Beat in sugar, vanilla and eggs. Stir in remaining ingredients except malted milk balls.

Spread batter in pan. Sprinkle with malted milk balls. Bake 30 to 35 minutes or until toothpick inserted in center comes out clean. Cool completely. **48 brownies.**

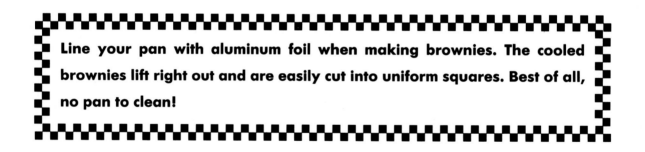

Line your pan with aluminum foil when making brownies. The cooled brownies lift right out and are easily cut into uniform squares. Best of all, no pan to clean!

AMARETTO BROWNIES

⅔ cup blanched almonds, toasted

8 ounces semisweet chocolate

⅓ cup margarine or butter

1¼ cups all-purpose flour

1 cup sugar

2 tablespoons amaretto

1 teaspoon baking powder

½ teaspoon salt

2 eggs

Amaretto Frosting (below)

Heat oven to 350°. Grease rectangular pan, 13 × 9 × 2 inches. Place ⅓ cup almonds in food processor. Cover and process, using quick on-and-off motions, until almonds are ground. Chop remaining almonds; reserve. Heat chocolate and margarine in 3-quart saucepan over low heat, stirring frequently, until melted; remove from heat. Stir in ground almonds and remaining ingredients except Amaretto Frosting and chopped almonds.

Spread batter in pan. Bake 22 to 27 minutes or until toothpick inserted in center comes out clean. Cool completely. Prepare Amaretto Frosting and spread on brownies; sprinkle with reserved chopped almonds. **32 brownies.**

AMARETTO FROSTING

2 cups powdered sugar

3 tablespoons margarine or butter, softened

1 tablespoon amaretto

1 to 2 tablespoons milk

Mix all ingredients until smooth.

MOCHA BROWNIES

A wonderfully sophisticated blend of coffee and chocolate, these brownies are like little filled cakes. Be sure to try the coconut and raspberry variations.

2 ounces unsweetened chocolate

½ cup margarine or butter

¾ cup all-purpose flour

¾ cup sugar

1 tablespoon instant coffee crystals

2 tablespoons milk

½ teaspoon baking powder

¼ teaspoon salt

2 eggs

Mocha Filling (below)

Chocolate Glaze (below)

Heat oven to 350°. Grease square pan, 8 × 8 × 2 inches. Heat chocolate and margarine in 2-quart saucepan over low heat, stirring frequently, until melted; remove from heat. Stir in remaining ingredients except Mocha Filling and Chocolate Glaze.

Spread batter in pan. Bake 18 to 22 minutes or until toothpick inserted in center comes out clean. Cool completely. Prepare Mocha Filling and spread on brownies. Prepare Chocolate Glaze and drizzle on filling. **16 brownies.**

MOCHA FILLING

2 teaspoons freeze-dried instant coffee

1 tablespoon very hot water

2 cups powdered sugar

2 tablespoons margarine or butter, softened

2 to 3 teaspoons water

Dissolve instant coffee in water in medium bowl. Stir in remaining ingredients until smooth.

CHOCOLATE GLAZE

¼ cup semisweet chocolate chips

1 teaspoon shortening

Heat chocolate and shortening in 1-quart saucepan over low heat, stirring constantly, until melted and smooth.

Coconut Brownies: Omit instant coffee from brownies. Omit Mocha Filling. Mix together 1½ cups powdered sugar, ½ cup shredded or flaked coconut, 2 tablespoons softened margarine and 2 tablespoons milk. Continue as directed using coconut filling.

Raspberry Brownies: Omit instant coffee and add ¼ teaspoon almond extract to brownies. Omit Mocha Filling. Spread ¼ cup red raspberry preserves over cooled brownies. Drizzle with glaze made with chocolate or vanilla milk chips.

Mocha Brownies, Coconut Brownies, Raspberry Brownies

German Chocolate Brownies

2 bars (4 ounces each) sweet cooking chocolate

½ cup margarine or butter

1½ cups all-purpose flour

1 cup sugar

½ teaspoon baking powder

½ teaspoon vanilla

¼ teaspoon salt

2 eggs

Coconut-Pecan Frosting (below)

Heat oven to 350°. Grease rectangular pan, 13 × 9 × 2 inches. Heat chocolate and margarine in 3-quart saucepan over low heat, stirring frequently, until melted; remove from heat. Stir in remaining ingredients except Coconut-Pecan Frosting.

Spread batter in pan. Bake 20 to 25 minutes or until toothpick inserted in center comes out clean. Cool completely. Prepare Coconut-Pecan Frosting and spread on brownies. **32 brownies.**

Coconut-Pecan Frosting

½ cup sugar

¼ cup margarine or butter

⅓ cup evaporated milk

½ teaspoon vanilla

2 egg yolks

1 cup flaked coconut

⅔ cup chopped pecans

Mix sugar, margarine, milk, vanilla and egg yolks in 1½-quart saucepan. (Margarine will remain lumpy.) Cook over medium heat about 12 minutes, stirring frequently, until thick. Stir in coconut and pecans. Beat until of spreading consistency.

German Chocolate Brownies, Cream Cheese Brownies (page 172), Vanilla Brownies (pages 172–173)

BAKE SALE

CREAM CHEESE BROWNIES

**4 squares (1 ounce each) unsweetened
   chocolate**

1 cup margarine or butter

Cream Cheese Filling (below)

2 cups sugar

2 teaspoons vanilla

4 eggs

1½ cups all-purpose flour

½ teaspoon salt

1 cup coarsely chopped nuts

Heat oven to 350°. Grease rectangular pan, 13 × 9 × 2 inches. Heat chocolate and margarine over low heat, stirring frequently, until melted; remove from heat. Cool. Prepare Cream Cheese Filling; reserve. Beat chocolate mixture, sugar, vanilla and eggs in large bowl on medium speed 1 minute, scraping bowl occasionally. Beat in flour and salt on low speed 30 seconds, scraping bowl occasionally. Beat on medium speed 1 minute. Stir in nuts.

Spread half of the batter (about 2½ cups) in pan. Spread with filling. Carefully spread remaining batter over filling. Bake 45 to 50 minutes or until toothpick inserted in center comes out clean. Cool completely. Refrigerate any remaining brownies. **48 brownies.**

CREAM CHEESE FILLING

**2 packages (8 ounces each) cream cheese,
   softened**

½ cup sugar

2 teaspoons vanilla

1 egg

Beat all ingredients until smooth.

VANILLA BROWNIES

Vanilla extract, glaze and creamy chips give these moist bars rich vanilla flavor.

**1 package (10 ounces) vanilla milk chips
   (1⅔ cups)**

½ cup margarine or butter

1¼ cups all-purpose flour

¾ cup sugar

½ cup chopped nuts

1 teaspoon vanilla

¼ teaspoon salt

3 eggs

Vanilla Glaze (page 173)

Heat oven to 350°. Grease and flour rectangular pan, 13 × 9 × 2 inches. Heat vanilla chips and margarine in heavy 2-quart saucepan over low heat, stirring frequently, just until melted. (Mixture may appear curdled.) Remove from heat; cool. Stir in remaining ingredients except Vanilla Glaze.

Spread batter in pan. Bake 30 to 35 minutes or until toothpick inserted in center comes out clean. Cool completely. Prepare Vanilla Glaze and spread on brownies. **32 brownies.**

Vanilla Glaze

1½ cups powdered sugar

3 tablespoons margarine or butter, softened

1 to 2 tablespoons milk

½ teaspoon vanilla

Mix all ingredients until smooth.

Peanut Butter Swirl Brownies

The "hills" created when the knife is drawn through the batter to make a swirl effect level off while the brownies bake.

⅔ cup granulated sugar

½ cup packed brown sugar

½ cup margarine or butter, softened

2 tablespoons milk

2 eggs

¾ cup all-purpose flour

½ teaspoon baking powder

¼ teaspoon salt

¼ cup peanut butter

⅓ cup peanut butter–flavored chips

⅓ cup cocoa

⅓ cup semisweet chocolate chips

Heat oven to 350°. Grease square pan, 9 × 9 × 2 inches. Mix sugars, margarine, milk and eggs in large bowl. Stir in flour, baking powder and salt. Divide batter in half (about 1 cup plus 2 tablespoons for each half). Stir peanut butter and peanut butter chips into one half. Stir cocoa and chocolate chips into remaining half.

Spoon chocolate batter into pan in 8 mounds, checkerboard style. Spoon peanut butter batter between mounds of chocolate batter. Gently swirl knife through batter for marbled effect. Bake 30 to 35 minutes or until toothpick inserted in center comes out clean. Cool completely. **16 brownies.**

Chapter Nine
Bar Cookies

▼▼▼▼▼▼▼▼▼▼▼▼▼▼▼▼▼▼▼▼▼▼▼▼▼▼

For a simply prepared, no-fuss cookie, we think a bar may be your best bet. Bar cookies are easy because you spread the batter in the pan, bake and cut into portions. But, don't imagine that bar cookies are humdrum! They can be exotic or homey, from Linzer Torte Bars (page 176) to Double Apple Bars (page 179).

▼▼▼▼▼▼▼▼▼▼▼▼▼▼▼▼▼▼▼▼▼▼▼▼▼▼

THE ULTIMATE
Date Bar

Date Filling (below)

1 cup margarine or butter, softened

1 cup packed brown sugar

1¾ cups all-purpose flour

1½ cups quick-cooking or old-fashioned oats

½ teaspoon salt

½ teaspoon baking soda

Prepare Date Filling; cool. Heat oven to 400°. Mix margarine and brown sugar in large bowl until well blended. Stir in remaining ingredients. Press half of the mixture in ungreased rectangular pan, 13 × 9 × 2 inches. Spread with filling or 1 cup of jam. Top with remaining crumbly mixture. Press lightly. Bake 25 to 30 minutes or until light brown. Cool 30 minutes. Cut into bars while warm. **32 bars.**

DATE FILLING
1½ cups water

¼ cup sugar

2 packages (8 ounces each) dates, chopped

Cook all ingredients over low heat, stirring until thickened.

▼▼▼▼▼▼▼▼▼▼▼▼▼▼▼▼▼▼▼▼▼▼▼▼▼▼

The Ultimate Date Bar, Lemon Squares (page 176), Cherry-Almond Bars (page 178)

Lemon Squares

1 cup all-purpose flour

½ cup margarine or butter, softened

¼ cup powdered sugar

1 cup granulated sugar

2 tablespoons lemon juice

2 teaspoons grated lemon peel, if desired

½ teaspoon baking powder

¼ teaspoon salt

2 eggs

Heat oven to 350°. Mix flour, margarine and powdered sugar. Press in ungreased square pan, 8 × 8 × 2 or 9 × 9 × 2 inches, building up ½-inch edge. Bake 20 minutes.

Beat remaining ingredients on high speed about 3 minutes or until light and fluffy. Pour over baked layer. Bake 25 to 30 minutes longer or just until almost no indentation remains when touched lightly in center. Cool completely. Sprinkle with powdered sugar. **25 squares.**

Linzer Torte Bars

To cut the bars into triangles, first cut into squares, then cut each square diagonally in half.

1 cup all-purpose flour

1 cup powdered sugar

1 cup ground walnuts

½ cup margarine or butter, softened

½ teaspoon ground cinnamon

⅔ cup red raspberry preserves

Heat oven to 375°. Mix all ingredients except preserves until crumbly. Press two-thirds of mixture in ungreased square pan, 9 × 9 × 2 inches. Spread with preserves. Sprinkle with remaining crumbs. Press gently into preserves. Bake 20 to 25 minutes or until light golden brown. Cool completely. **48 bars.**

Apricot Linzer Bars: Substitute ground almonds for the ground walnuts and apricot preserves for the raspberry preserves.

Linzer Torte Bars

CHERRY-ALMOND BARS

Like the Linzer Torte Bars, these too can easily be cut into triangles.

1 cup all-purpose flour

½ cup margarine or butter, softened

¼ cup powdered sugar

2 eggs

1 cup sliced almonds

½ cup granulated sugar

¼ cup all-purpose flour

½ teaspoon baking powder

1 jar (10 ounces) maraschino cherries, drained, chopped and juice reserved

Pink Glaze (below)

Heat oven to 350°. Mix 1 cup flour, the margarine and powdered sugar. Press in ungreased square pan, 9 × 9 × 2 inches. Bake 10 minutes or until set.

Beat eggs in medium bowl. Stir in remaining ingredients except Pink Glaze. Spread over baked layer. Bake 20 to 25 minutes or until golden brown. Cool completely. Prepare Pink Glaze and drizzle on bars. **24 bars.**

PINK GLAZE

½ cup powdered sugar

2 to 3 teaspoons reserved maraschino cherry juice

¼ teaspoon almond extract

Mix all ingredients until smooth and of desired consistency.

PEANUT BUTTER AND JAM BARS

½ cup granulated sugar

½ cup packed brown sugar

½ cup shortening

½ cup peanut butter

1 egg

1¼ cups all-purpose flour

¾ teaspoon baking soda

½ teaspoon baking powder

½ cup red raspberry jam

Glaze (page 179)

Heat oven to 350°. Mix sugars, shortening, peanut butter and egg in large bowl. Stir in flour, baking soda and baking powder.

Reserve 1 cup dough. Press remaining dough in ungreased rectangular pan, 13 × 9 × 2 inches. Spread with jam. Crumble reserved dough and sprinkle over jam. Bake 20 to 25 minutes or until golden brown. Cool completely. Prepare Glaze and drizzle on bars. **32 bars.**

GLAZE

2 tablespoons margarine or butter

1 cup powdered sugar

1 teaspoon vanilla

3 to 4 teaspoons hot water

Heat margarine in 1-quart saucepan over low heat until melted; remove from heat. Mix in powdered sugar and vanilla. Beat in water, 1 teaspoon at a time, until smooth and of desired consistency.

DOUBLE APPLE BARS

To serve as dessert, cut into 16 squares and serve with cinnamon or vanilla ice cream.

¾ cup packed brown sugar

¾ cup applesauce

¼ cup vegetable oil

1 egg

1¼ cups all-purpose flour

½ teaspoon baking soda

½ teaspoon ground cinnamon

¼ teaspoon salt

½ cup chopped unpared all-purpose apple

Powdered sugar

Heat oven to 350°. Mix brown sugar, applesauce, oil and egg in large bowl. Stir in flour, baking soda, cinnamon and salt. Stir in apple.

Spread batter in ungreased square pan, 9 × 9 × 2 inches. Bake 25 to 30 minutes or until toothpick inserted in center comes out clean. Cool. Sprinkle with powdered sugar. **24 bars.**

BANANA-NUT BARS

1 cup sugar

1 cup mashed ripe bananas (about 3 medium)

⅓ cup vegetable oil

2 eggs

1 cup all-purpose flour

1 teaspoon baking powder

½ teaspoon baking soda

½ teaspoon ground cinnamon

¼ teaspoon salt

½ cup chopped nuts

Cream Cheese Frosting (below)

Heat oven to 350°. Grease rectangular pan, 13 × 9 × 2 inches. Beat sugar, bananas, oil and eggs in large bowl. Stir in flour, baking powder, baking soda, cinnamon and salt. Stir in nuts.

Spread batter in pan. Bake 25 to 30 minutes or until toothpick inserted in center comes out clean. Cool completely. Prepare Cream Cheese Frosting and spread on bars. Cover and refrigerate any remaining bars. **24 bars.**

CREAM CHEESE FROSTING

1 package (3 ounces) cream cheese, softened

⅓ cup margarine or butter, softened

1 teaspoon vanilla

2 cups powdered sugar

Beat cream cheese, margarine and vanilla in medium bowl on low speed until smooth. Gradually beat in powdered sugar until smooth.

Top: Pumpkin-Spice Bars (page 182), Middle: Zucchini Bars (page 182), Bottom: Banana-Nut Bars

Zucchini Bars

⅔ cup packed brown sugar

¼ cup margarine or butter, softened

1 egg

½ teaspoon vanilla

1 cup all-purpose flour

1 teaspoon baking soda

½ teaspoon ground cinnamon

½ teaspoon ground cloves

1 cup shredded zucchini, drained

½ cup chopped nuts

Spice Frosting (below)

Heat oven to 350°. Grease square pan, 8 × 8 × 2 or 9 × 9 × 2 inches. Mix brown sugar, margarine, egg and vanilla in large bowl. Stir in flour, baking soda, cinnamon and cloves. Stir in zucchini and nuts.

Spread batter in pan. Bake 25 to 30 minutes or until toothpick inserted in center comes out clean. Cool completely. Prepare Spice Frosting and spread on bars. **24 bars.**

Spice Frosting

¾ cup powdered sugar

1 tablespoon margarine or butter, softened

3 to 4 teaspoons milk

⅛ teaspoon ground cloves

Mix all ingredients until smooth and of spreading consistency.

Pumpkin Spice Bars

4 eggs

2 cups sugar

1 cup vegetable oil

1 can (16 ounces) pumpkin

2 cups all-purpose flour

2 teaspoons baking powder

2 teaspoons ground cinnamon

1 teaspoon baking soda

½ teaspoon salt

½ teaspoon ground ginger

¼ teaspoon ground cloves

1 cup raisins

Cream Cheese Frosting (page 180)

½ cup chopped nuts

Heat oven to 350°. Grease jelly roll pan, 15½ × 10½ × 1 inch. Beat eggs, sugar, oil and pumpkin in large bowl. Stir in flour, baking powder, cinnamon, baking soda, salt, ginger and cloves. Stir in raisins.

Pour batter into pan. Bake 25 to 30 minutes or until toothpick inserted in center comes out clean. Cool completely. Prepare Cream Cheese Frosting and spread on bars; sprinkle with nuts. **48 bars.**

CINNAMON-COFFEE BARS

Cold coffee can be substituted for the milk in the glaze. It will add subtle coffee flavor and light tan color.

1 cup packed brown sugar

⅓ cup margarine or butter, softened

1 egg

1½ cups all-purpose flour

½ cup raisins

¼ cup chopped nuts

½ cup water

1 tablespoon freeze-dried instant coffee

1 teaspoon baking powder

½ teaspoon cinnamon

¼ teaspoon salt

¼ teaspoon baking soda

Glaze (below)

Heat oven to 350°. Grease and flour rectangular pan, 13 × 9 × 2 inches. Mix brown sugar, margarine and egg in large bowl. Stir in remaining ingredients except Glaze.

Spread batter in pan. Bake 20 to 22 minutes or until top springs back when touched in center. Prepare Glaze and drizzle on warm bars. Cool. **32 bars.**

GLAZE

1 cup powdered sugar

4 to 5 teaspoons milk

¼ teaspoon vanilla

Mix ingredients until smooth and of desired consistency.

Fudge Meltaway Squares

½ cup margarine or butter

1½ squares unsweetened chocolate

1¾ cups graham cracker crumbs

1 cup flaked coconut

½ cup chopped nuts

¼ cup granulated sugar

2 tablespoons water

1 teaspoon vanilla

2 cups powdered sugar

¼ cup margarine or butter, softened

2 tablespoons milk

1 teaspoon vanilla

1½ squares unsweetened chocolate

Line square pan, 9 × 9 × 2 inches, with aluminum foil. Heat ½ cup margarine and 1½ squares chocolate in 3-quart saucepan over low heat, stirring occasionally, until melted; remove from heat. Stir in graham cracker crumbs, coconut, nuts, granulated sugar, water and 1 teaspoon vanilla. Press in pan. Refrigerate.

Mix remaining ingredients except 1½ squares unsweetened chocolate. Spread over refrigerated crumb mixture. Refrigerate 15 minutes. Heat chocolate until melted. Drizzle over frosted bars. Refrigerate 2 hours or until almost hard. Remove squares, along with foil, from pan. Fold foil back to cut squares. Cover and refrigerate any remaining squares. **36 squares.**

Toffee Bars

For a change of shape, cut into triangles or diamonds.

1 cup margarine or butter, softened

1 cup packed brown sugar

1 egg yolk

1 teaspoon vanilla

2 cups all-purpose flour

¼ teaspoon salt

1 bar (4 ounces) milk chocolate candy, broken into pieces

½ cup chopped nuts

Heat oven to 350°. Mix margarine, brown sugar, egg yolk and vanilla in large bowl. Stir in flour and salt.

Press dough in ungreased rectangular pan, 13 × 9 × 2 inches. Bake 25 to 30 minutes or until very light brown. (Crust will be soft.) Immediately place milk chocolate pieces on baked layer. Let stand about 5 minutes or until soft; spread evenly. Sprinkle with nuts. Cool 30 minutes. Cut into bars while warm. **32 bars.**

Mousse Bars

1½ cups vanilla wafer crumbs (about 40 wafers)

¼ cup margarine or butter, melted

¾ cup whipping (heavy) cream

1 package (6 ounces) semisweet chocolate chips (1 cup)

3 eggs

⅓ cup sugar

⅛ teaspoon salt

Chocolate Topping (below)

Heat oven to 350°. Mix wafer crumbs and margarine. Press in ungreased square pan, 8 × 8 × 2 or 9 × 9 × 2 inches. Bake 10 minutes.

Heat whipping cream and chocolate chips over low heat, stirring frequently, until chocolate is melted; remove from heat. Cool about 5 minutes. Beat eggs, sugar and salt in large bowl until foamy. Pour chocolate mixture into egg mixture, stirring constantly. Pour over baked layer in pan. Bake 25 to 35 minutes or until center springs back when touched lightly. Cool 15 minutes. Prepare Chocolate Topping and spread on bars. Refrigerate uncovered 2 hours or until chilled. **16 bars.**

Chocolate Topping

½ cup semisweet chocolate chips

1 tablespoon shortening

Heat chocolate chips and shortening over low heat, stirring frequently, until melted.

Left: *Fudge Meltaway Squares (page 184)*, Top: *Mousse Bars (page 185)*, Bottom: *Toffee Bars (page 184)*

DREAM BARS

⅓ cup margarine or butter, softened

⅓ cup packed brown sugar

1 cup all-purpose flour

Almond-Coconut Topping (below)

Heat oven to 350°. Mix margarine and brown sugar in medium bowl until well blended. Stir in flour. Press mixture in ungreased rectangular pan, 13 × 9 × 2 inches. Bake 10 minutes. Prepare Almond-Coconut Topping.

Spread topping on partially baked bars. Bake 20 to 25 minutes longer or until topping is golden brown. Cool 30 minutes. Cut into bars while warm. **32 bars.**

ALMOND-COCONUT TOPPING

2 eggs

1 cup shredded coconut

1 cup chopped almonds

¾ cup packed brown sugar

2 tablespoons all-purpose flour

1 teaspoon baking powder

1 teaspoon vanilla

¼ teaspoon salt

Beat eggs in medium bowl. Stir in remaining ingredients.

CREAM-FILLED OAT BARS

Wonderfully creamy in the center, these golden brown cookies are an exceptional treat.

1 can (14 ounces) sweetened condensed milk

2 teaspoons grated lemon peel

¼ cup lemon juice

1¼ cups all-purpose flour

1 cup quick-cooking or old-fashioned oats

½ cup packed brown sugar

½ cup margarine or butter, softened

¼ teaspoon salt

¼ teaspoon baking soda

Heat oven to 375°. Grease square pan, 9 × 9 × 2 inches. Mix milk, lemon peel and lemon juice until thickened; reserve. Mix remaining ingredients until crumbly.

Press half of the crumbly mixture in pan. Bake about 10 minutes or until set. Spread milk mixture over baked layer. Sprinkle remaining crumbly mixture on milk mixture. Press gently into milk mixture. Bake about 20 minutes or until edge is golden brown and center is set but soft. Cool completely. **24 bars.**

Cream-filled Oat Bars, Caramel Candy Bars (page 190)

CARAMEL CANDY BARS

1 package (14 ounces) vanilla caramels

⅓ cup milk

2 cups all-purpose flour

2 cups quick-cooking or old-fashioned oats

1½ cups packed brown sugar

1 teaspoon baking soda

½ teaspoon salt

1 egg

1 cup margarine or butter, softened

1 package (6 ounces) semisweet chocolate chips (1 cup)

1 cup chopped walnuts or dry roasted peanuts

Heat oven to 350°. Heat caramels and milk in 2-quart saucepan over low heat, stirring frequently, until smooth; remove from heat and reserve. Mix flour, oats, brown sugar, baking soda and salt in large bowl. Stir in egg and margarine with fork until mixture is crumbly.

Press half of the crumbly mixture in ungreased rectangular pan, 13 × 9 × 2 inches. Bake 10 minutes. Sprinkle with chocolate chips and walnuts. Drizzle with caramel mixture. Sprinkle remaining crumbly mixture over top. Bake 20 to 25 minutes or until golden brown. Cool 30 minutes. Loosen edges from sides of pan. Cool completely. **48 bars.**

MIXED NUT BARS

1 cup margarine or butter, softened

1 cup packed brown sugar

1 egg yolk

1 teaspoon vanilla

2 cups all-purpose flour

¼ teaspoon salt

8 ounces vanilla flavor candy coating, chopped, or 1¼ cups vanilla milk chips

1 can (12 ounces) salted mixed nuts

Heat oven to 350°. Mix margarine, brown sugar, egg yolk and vanilla in large bowl. Stir in flour and salt.

Press mixture in ungreased rectangular pan, 13 × 9 × 2 inches. Bake about 25 minutes or until light brown. Immediately sprinkle candy coating evenly on baked layer. Let stand about 5 minutes or until soft; spread evenly. Sprinkle with nuts; gently press into topping. Cool completely. **32 bars.**

COCONUT MACAROON BARS

Here is a cookie that tastes just like a chocolate-covered coconut candy bar.

¾ cup all-purpose flour

¼ cup powdered sugar

¼ cup margarine or butter, softened

½ teaspoon almond extract

1 egg yolk

1 cup chopped walnuts

1 can (14 ounces) sweetened condensed milk

1 package (7 ounces) flaked coconut (about 2⅔ cups)

½ cup semisweet chocolate chips

Heat oven to 350°. Grease square pan, 9 × 9 × 2 inches. Mix flour, powdered sugar, margarine, almond extract and egg yolk. (Mixture will be crumbly.) Press in pan. Bake 12 to 15 minutes or until edges are light brown and center is set.

Mix walnuts, milk and coconut. Spread over baked layer. Bake 25 to 30 minutes or until golden brown. Immediately sprinkle chocolate chips evenly on baked layer. Let stand about 5 minutes or until soft; spread carefully. Refrigerate uncovered 1 to 2 hours or until chocolate is set. **24 bars.**

Pecan Pie Squares

3 cups all-purpose flour

⅓ cup sugar

¾ cup margarine or butter, softened

½ teaspoon salt

Filling (below)

Heat oven to 350°. Grease jelly roll pan, 15½ × 10½ × 1 inch. Beat flour, sugar, margarine and salt in large bowl on low speed until crumbly. (Mixture will be dry.) Press firmly in pan. Bake about 20 minutes or until light golden brown.

Prepare Filling and pour over baked layer; spread evenly. Bake about 25 minutes or until filling is set. Cool completely. **60 squares.**

Filling

1½ cups sugar

1½ cups corn syrup

3 tablespoons margarine or butter, melted

1½ teaspoons vanilla

4 eggs, slightly beaten

2½ cups chopped pecans

Mix all ingredients except pecans in large bowl until well blended. Stir in pecans.

Pecan Pie Squares

NO-BAKE—PEANUT BUTTER SQUARES

2 cups powdered sugar

1 cup margarine or butter, softened

1 cup peanut butter

1 teaspoon vanilla

2¾ cups graham cracker crumbs

1 cup chopped peanuts

1 package (12 ounces) semisweet chocolate chips (2 cups)

¼ cup peanut butter

Line square pan, 9 × 9 × 2 inches, with aluminum foil. Mix powdered sugar, margarine, 1 cup peanut butter and the vanilla in large bowl. Stir in graham cracker crumbs and peanuts. (Mixture will be stiff.) Press in pan.

Heat chocolate chips and ¼ cup peanut butter over low heat, stirring frequently, until smooth. Spread over bars. Refrigerate 1 hour or until chocolate is set. Remove squares, along with foil, from pan. Fold foil back to cut squares. Refrigerate 2 hours or until firm. Cover and refrigerate any remaining squares. **36 squares.**

NO-BAKE HONEY-OAT BARS

A nice mix of honey, fruit and cinnamon, these are like homemade chewy granola bars.

¼ cup sugar

¼ cup margarine or butter

⅓ cup honey

½ teaspoon ground cinnamon

1 cup dried fruit bits

1½ cups whole wheat flake cereal

1 cup quick-cooking oats

½ cup sliced almonds

Butter square pan, 9 × 9 × 2 inches. Heat sugar, margarine, honey and cinnamon in 3-quart saucepan over medium heat, stirring constantly, until boiling. Boil 1 minute, stirring constantly; remove from heat. Stir in fruit bits. Stir in remaining ingredients. Press mixture in pan with back of wooden spoon. Cool completely. **24 bars.**

No-bake–Peanut Butter Squares, No-Bake Honey-Oat Bars

CANADIAN METRIC CONVERSION TABLES

*Dry and Liquid Measurements

IMPERIAL	METRIC
¼ teaspoon	1 mL
½ teaspoon	2 mL
1 teaspoon	5 mL
1 tablespoon	15 mL
2 tablespoons	25 mL
3 tablespoons	50 mL
¼ cup	50 mL
⅓ cup	75 mL
½ cup	125 mL
⅔ cup	150 mL
¾ cup	175 mL
1 cup	250 mL

Temperatures

FAHRENHEIT	CELSIUS
32°F	0°C
212°F	100°C
250°F	121°C
275°F	140°C
300°F	150°C
325°F	160°C
350°F	180°C
375°F	190°C
400°F	200°C
425°F	220°C
450°F	230°C
475°F	240°C

*Common Cooking & Baking Utensil Equivalents

BAKEWARE	IMPERIAL	METRIC
Round Pan	8 × 1½ inches	20 × 4 cm
	9 × 1½ inches	22 × 4 cm
Square Pan	8 × 8 × 2 inches	22 × 22 × 5 cm
	9 × 9 × 2 inches	23 × 23 × 5 cm
Baking Dishes	11 × 7 × 1½ inches	28 × 18 × 4 cm
	12 × 7½ × 2 inches	30 × 19 × 5 cm
	13 × 9 × 2 inches	33 × 23 × 5 cm
Loaf Pan	8½ × 4½ × 2½ inches	22 × 11 × 6 cm
	9 × 5 × 3 inches	23 × 13 × 8 cm
Tube Pan	10 × 4 inches	25 × 10 cm
Jelly Roll Pan	15½ × 10½ × 1 inch	39 × 27 × 2.5 cm
Pie Plate	9 × 1¼ inches	23 × 3.2 cm
	10 × 1½ inches	25 × 4 cm
Muffin Cups	2½ × 1¼ inches	6 × 3.2 cm
	3 × 1½ inches	8 × 4 cm
Skillet	10 inches	25 cm
Casseroles and	1 quart	1 L
Saucepans	1½ quarts	1.5 L
	2 quarts	2 L
	2½ quarts	2.5 L
	3 quarts	3 L
	4 quarts	4 L

Note: The recipes in this cookbook have not been developed or tested in Canadian metric measures. When converting recipes to Canadian metric, some variations in quality may be noted.

*Based on the U.S. System of Weights and Measures.

INDEX

Index

Index

CREDITS

PRENTICE HALL

Publisher: Nina D. Hoffman
Executive Editor: Rebecca W. Atwater
Editor: Anne Ficklen
Assistant Editor: Rachel Simon
Assistant Art Director: Frederick J. Latasa
Photographic Director: Carmen Bonilla
Illustrator: Laurie Lee Davis
Senior Production Manager: Susan Joseph
Assistant Managing Editor: Kimberly Ann Ebert

GENERAL MILLS, INC.

Senior Editor: Karen Couné
Recipe Development and Testing: Mary Hallin Johnson, Linel Reiber, Julie H. Turnbull, Diane Undis
Recipe Copy Editor: Deb Hance
Editorial Assistant: Elaine Mitchell
Food Stylists: Kate Courtney, Mary Sethre, Cindy Lund
Photographer: Nanci Doonan Dixon
Photography Assistant: Scott Wyberg
Director, Betty Crocker Food and Publications Center: Marcia Copeland
Assistant Manager, Publications: Lois Tlusty

Betty Crocker

75POINTS

SAVE these Betty Crocker Points and redeem them for big savings on hundreds of kitchen, home, gift and children's items! For catalog, send 50¢ with your name and address to: General Mills, P.O. Box 5389, Mpls., MN 55460.

Redeemable with cash in USA before May 1999. Void where prohibited, taxed or regulated.

S

CUT OUT AND SAVE